LIVING UNDER THATCH
Vernacular architecture in Co. Offaly

LIVING UNDER THATCH

Vernacular architecture in Co. Offaly

BARRY O'REILLY

MERCIER PRESS

MERCIER PRESS
Douglas Village, Cork
www.mercierpress.ie

Trade enquiries to COLUMBA MERCIER DISTRIBUTION,
55a Spruce Avenue, Stillorgan Industrial Park, Blackrock, Dublin

1 85635 429 6

10 9 8 7 6 5 4 3 2 1

FOR JEAN AND LITTLE DOIREANN

This book is a project led by the Offaly Historical and Archaeological Society, as partners in the Offaly Heritage Forum and has been supported by Offaly Historical and Archaeological Society, Offaly County Council, the Heritage Council and the Offaly LEADER + Company.

  SUPPORTED BY THE HERITAGE COUNCIL

LE CUIDIÚ AN CHOMHAIRLE OIDHREACHTA   Offaly LEADER+ Company

Offaly Historical and   Offaly County Council
Archaeological Society

This project acknowledges the support of the Offaly LEADER + Company and the LEADER + Programme which is funded by the Irish Government and part-financed by the European Union under the National Development Plan 2000– 2006.

Printed in Ireland by ColourBooks Ltd

CONTENTS

FOREWORD

This book marks an important departure in Offaly where we have systematically examined an important area of our heritage and are marking it, in part, with this significant publication. The author has provided a profile of thatch in Offaly, which gives us an accurate picture of thatch at the beginning of a new century, contrasting this image with what has gone before. But it is also a practical guide, providing invaluable advice to owners of thatch and those thinking of investing in thatch. The challenges for thatch in the years ahead are clearly laid out and seek a response from many players, not just the owners. These challenges must be addressed in the years to come if we are to retain thatch as part of our heritage and as part of the landscape and not merely historically documented in these pages.

There is no doubt but that we have been fortunate in working with Barry O'Reilly who carried out the survey and who wrote this book. His knowledge and appreciation of thatch is second to none and, as always, it is a pleasure to work with someone who knows their subject so well. We have also been fortunate to work with Mary Feehan of Mercier Press who has been so professional in guiding this book to the bookshelves.

The book is also significant in that it is a result of the work of the Offaly Heritage Forum, spearheaded by the Offaly Historical and Archaeological Society. The Offaly Heritage Forum has brought together many of the key players in this area, first to plan and execute the detailed survey of thatch in Offaly in 2002 and then to follow this up with the aim of bringing this information to a wider audience through this book in 2004.

NIALL SWEENEY
Offaly County Manager

ACKNOWLEDGMENTS

I would like to specially thank the following:
Amanda Pedlow and Lisa Henry, Heritage Office, Offaly County Council. Offaly Heritage Forum. Brian Mahon, Geashill. Críostóir Mac Cárthaigh, Department of Irish Folklore, University College Dublin. Jimmy Lenehan, thatcher. Mary Hanna, The Heritage Council. Caimin O'Brien, Archaeological Survey of Ireland. Emmet Dolan, Séamus Conroy and Larry Hackett, thatchers. My wife, Jean Farrelly, for her great forbearance and for her editing skills. Mary Feehan and the staff at Mercier Press.

Thatch owners and former thatch owners to whom I am greatly indebted:
Seán Blanc, Clonmore, Clonbullogue. John and Tommy Boyle, Rathure South, Killyon. Paddy Bracken, Ballinvoher, Clonygowan. Kieran Brennan and family, Aghanannagh, Tullamore. Dorenda Buckley, Ballycue, Geashill. Frank Clarke, Cloghan. Chris Colligan, Derrybeg, Killeigh. Des Connole, Crinkill. Mary Coughlan, Annaghmore, Belmont. John Joe Coyne, Clonavoe, Clonbullogue. Paddy and Betty Dempsey, Urney, Clonygowan. Noel Devery, Turraun, Pollagh. Bridget Dooley, Broughal, Kilcormac. John Dunne, Derrybeg, Killeigh. Mary Dunne, Bracklin Little, Derrygolan. Joe Feeney, Killeenmore, Killeigh. Mary Jane Fox, Ballytoran, Shinrone. Mary Galvin and family, Bogtown. Vera Galvin, Knockballyboy, Daingean. Mary Garahy, Derrinduff, Crinkill. Garry family, Ballykean, Geashill. Ernest Gowing, Cappancur, Tullamore. Francis Griffith, Ballybruncullin, Ballycumber. Mary Grimes, Loughroe, Rahan. Harry Gunning, Stonestown, Cloghan. Larry and George Hackett, Ballyduff South, Ballinagar. Janet Hollingshead and family, Garrymona, Walsh Island. Ned Horan, Ballaghanoher, Birr. Séamus Horan, Broughal, Kilcormac. John Howlin, Killurin. Ned Kavanagh, Coolcor, Rhode. Peter Kelly and family, Cloncon, Tullamore. Martin Langton, Killellery, Geashill. Pat and Helen Loonam, Kilcormac. Marian McDonald, Lavagh, Lusmagh. Kieran McIntyre, Galros, Cloghan. Joseph and Máiréad McKenna, Cloncoher, Newtown, Killeigh. Willie and Séamus Mahon, Coolnagrower, Crinkill. Cecilia Marshall, Ballyatty, Kilcolman. Paddy Meacle, Murragh, Rahan. Philip Minnock and family, Kilgortin, Rahan. Michael Molloy, Killurin and England. Tom Molloy, Lea More, Kilcormac. Percy Moyles, Kinnitty. Seán Murphy, Belmont. Noel and Mary O'Meara, Ballinagar. Chris O'Reilly, Tullamore. Daniel O'Shea, Enaghan, Walsh Island. Stephen Parker, Ferbane. Pádraic Plunkett, Killeenmore, Killeigh. Larry Rigney, Bawnmore, Geashill. Sam Rigney, Killaghintober, Ballycumber. Noel Ryan, Ballintemple, Cloughjordan. Ernie Skelly, Derryweelan, Geashill. Debbie Thomas, Ross, Tullamore. Jim and Philomena Tooher, Ballyegan, Birr.

Official and academic bodies:
Department of Irish Folklore, University College Dublin. Housing Grants Section, Department of the Environment, Heritage and Local Government. Irish Architectural Archive. Offaly Historical and Archaeological Society: Michael Byrne, John Kearney, Stephen McNeill and Noel Guerin. Offaly County Council Fire Service. Offaly County Council Library Service.

Other individuals who were of assistance:
Laura Claffey, Clonmacnoise. John and Paul Conlon (thatchers), Athlone, Co. Westmeath. Liam Marshall, Sharavogue. Kyran O'Grady (thatcher), Knockrobin, Co. Wicklow. Willie Cumming, National Inventory of Architectural Heritage. Austin O'Sullivan, Irish Agricultural Museum, Johnstown Castle, Co. Wexford. Sr Oliver Wrafter, Presentation Convent, Killina.

Battened (door): A door formed from vertical boards of timber and braced behind. Such boards may be narrow or wide. There may be a half-door of similar construction in front of the main door.

Bay: A 'bay' corresponds to an opening in the front wall of a building. A house with a door and three windows is said to be a 'four-bay house'.

Blade: A sloping timber forming part of a roof *truss*.

Collar: A horizontal timber that connects blades of an A-shaped couple or roof truss.

Couple truss: The A-shaped roof trusses in a vernacular building. They are usually quite widely spaced and often made of unsawn timbering.

Direct-entry (plan): Plan form typical of houses in western and upland areas of Ireland.

Jamb wall: A wall or partition which screens the kitchen hearth from draughts from an open front door and forms a lobby or small hall between itself and the front doorway in *lobby-entry* houses.

Lime-plaster: A wall rendering formed from lime, sand and water.

Lime-wash: A light wall rendering made from lime and water. A pigment may be added to produce a colour wash.

Lobby-entry (plan): Plan form typical of houses in eastern and lowland Ireland.

Record of Monuments and Places (RMP): The national list of archaeological sites and monuments.

Record of Protected Structures (RPS): List of buildings and sites of architectural importance in a county or town.

Ribs/ribberies: Light, usually unsawn timbers laid over the main roof timbers. Their main purpose is to support a scraw and/or the straw or reed in a thatched roof.

Ridgepole: The roof timber running along the ridge of a roof. It is often of quite slight dimensions. The upper end of the blades of a couple truss or the rafters of a 'modern' truss connect into it.

Sash (window): The typical 'up/down' window seen in older buildings. Older types tend to have smaller panes than more modern forms.

Scollop: A length of hazel or willow that is used for securing straw or reed in thatching.

Scolloped thatch: Thatching method that employs scollops for fixing thatch.

Scraw: A layer of sod from the top surface of a bog or from the surface of a grassy field. It is laid directly onto roof timbering to provide an anchorage for fixing thatch to a roof.

Spy window: A window often to be seen in a *jamb wall* of a lobby-entry house.

Stitching: Method of tying the under layer of straw or scraw to a roof structure, using straw rope fed through with a thatching needle.

Thatch: Any vegetable roof covering, most frequently of straw and reed – the most common and probably the oldest roofing material in the world.

Thrust thatch: Thatching method that usually foregoes a scraw under-thatch. The uppermost bundles of straw are thrust into the lower using a stick-like implement.

Truss: The basic component of most roof structures. Trusses occur in many different forms, but A-shaped are most common in vernacular roofs.

Vernacular: The term applied to the vast bulk of the world's architecture. Vernacular buildings are the work of 'ordinary' people as distinct from professional builders or architects and are the result of long-standing tradition rather than the drawing-board.

1

Vernacular Architecture: Ireland and the World

'Vernacular' architecture

All are familiar with the use of the term 'vernacular' to denote the everyday language of a people or community. Its origin lies in the Latin word *vernaculus* meaning a home-born slave and as applied to language came to describe the language of the 'ordinary' person as distinct from that of a ruling class or dominant outside power. Its application to architecture and specifically the buildings of a region, community or the 'ordinary people' dates back to the middle of the nineteenth century. The term is widely accepted internationally. Other words such as 'folk', 'peasant', 'everyday' and even 'traditional' are all less satisfactory and more ambiguous.

Kevin Danaher wrote:

> Ordinary people down through the ages and into recent and even modern times have continued to build their own houses, barns, stables and workshops and to develop them in their own way within their own resources to meet their own needs, unaffected in the main by trained architects, formal styles or fashionable trends. Thus emerged and evolved the vernacular architecture, the forms and methods which over the ages have become part of the living tradition of the ordinary people.[1]

The buildings created by 'ordinary people' are internationally regarded as being crucial to any understanding of the world's cultural heritage. It is worth quoting from the *Charter on the Built Vernacular Heritage*:

> The built vernacular heritage occupies a central place in the affection and pride of all peoples ... It appears informal, but nevertheless orderly. It is utilitarian and at the same time possesses remarkable beauty. It is a focus of contemporary life and at the same time a record of the history of society. It would be unworthy of the heritage of man if care is not taken to conserve these traditional harmonies which constitute the core of man's own existence.
>
> ... it is the fundamental expression of the culture of a community, of its relationship with its territories and, at the same time, the expression of the world's cultural diversity.
>
> ... The survival of this tradition is threatened world-wide by the forces of cultural homogenisation and industrial production.[2]

This declaration by ICOMOS should help to put the vernacular architecture of Ireland into its rightful international context. It also sums up much of what vernacular architecture is and also the many threats facing it. The owners of vernacular buildings, and the community in general, are seen to have a considerable responsibility in ensuring that such buildings and the skills to maintain them survive into the future. Stating that the diversity of the world's cultural heritage is at stake underlines the value of protecting our thatched houses and other expressions of the vernacular.

Ireland has been slow to appreciate its vernacular heritage. Although the first study took place in 1933, perhaps not unexpectedly by a foreigner, Ludwig Mulhausen,[3] the only substantial work has been by Alan Gailey whose book *Rural Houses of the North of Ireland* appeared in 1984.[4] There has been a trickle of studies and surveys through the years but little of it systematic or substantial and even less of the results appearing in print.

House with outbuilding under the same roof at Broughal, Kilcormac

Distinguishing between 'vernacular' and 'formal' architecture

In general, vernacular buildings can be contrasted with architect- or engineer-designed buildings. Vernacular architecture is 'architecture without architects'.[5] The labourer's cottage and latterly, the bungalow, have become the most common house types in the Irish landscape. It is worth commenting on the differences between these and the vernacular house.

Local authorities, the landed estates or the Board of Works designed the familiar and very widespread labourers' cottages.[6] They are superficially similar in size, form and simplicity to the vernacular house. Some of the estate cottages can be quite ornate, underlining their non-vernacular nature, a classic example of the latter is the village of Adare, Co. Limerick, whose thatched houses (more properly 'cottages') are arguably the best-known thatched houses on the island. The houses were, however, designed for the third Earl of Dunraven, an 'improving landlord' in the nineteenth century. The Swiss Cottage at Cahir, Co. Tipperary, a 'cottage ornée', also looks and indeed is exotic. The form of the windows and doors of these cot-

The Swiss Cottage at Cahir, Co. Tipperary

tages and their 'rustic' roofs are clearly not inspired by Irish vernacular houses. While the designers of formal cottages may have drawn some features from the traditional buildings of Ireland, these buildings are definitely the products of the designers.

The bungalow, which appears to have drawn considerably less from the vernacular than has the labourer's cottage, has often been stated, erroneously, to be 'today's vernacular'. While it is clear that the bungalow has admirably fulfilled the role of a comfortable and convenient house form, it is the result of formal, not traditional, design. The bulk of buildings in towns may be termed 'popular' or 'artisanal' architecture, having been designed by local builders, often as speculative ventures and some have even argued that Georgian houses might be regarded as vernacular since they were built often using local materials and by artisans from their locality. However, a glance at the table below should help to dispel this confusion.

Another characteristic of vernacular buildings that makes them distinct from formally designed buildings is the way they fit into the landscape. Their builders made the best use of available shelter from prevailing winds. It is very rare for vernacular buildings to be sited on elevated ground. The use of local materials gives such buildings a greater potential for blending into their setting, in contrast with more modern structures. An abandoned clay-walled building will, in time, return to the earth and constitutes 'bio-degradable' architecture. In an era of increasing consciousness concerning issues of sustainability, vernacular buildings embody the essence of 'environmental-friendliness'. Furthermore the use of older farming practices, tech-

	Vernacular Architecture	Formal Architecture
Builder	From immediate locality	Usually from some distance away
	Name rarely known	Name often known
Owner	Farmer, labourer, fisherman	Includes wealthy and professional people
	Often the builder	Rarely the builder
Scale	Relatively small buildings	Often much larger buildings
Costs	Relatively low	Usually considerably higher
Design	Drawn from tradition	Often designed professionally
	Simple shapes, roofs	Often complex shapes, roofs
	Thick walls	Usually much thinner walls
	Little ornamentation	Often ornamented, e.g., with carved bargeboards to gables
Inspiration	Tradition	Mainly influenced by architectural styles
	Strong regional character	Designs can usually be found anywhere
Climate & siting	Very carefully considered	Much less considered
Layout	One of two traditional plans	Can be of greatly differing type
	No formal hall	Usually a formal hall
	One room (pile) deep	Frequently two rooms (piles) deep
	Kitchen is hub of house	Kitchen is an ancillary room
	Small number of rooms	More rooms and more variety
Materials	From immediate locality	Often transported some distance
	Include mud, straw, wattle	Rarely use these materials
	Rarely include fired brick, cement and metals	Frequently include fired brick and cement, metals
	Often unsawn roof timbers	Usually sawn or at least squared timbers
	Rarely produced industrially	Often produced industrially
	Majority originally thatched	Thatch used rarely, as ornament
Survival	Heavily rural	Greater proportion is urban
Dating	Rarely datable	Usually a precise date known
	No longer built since c. 1900	Continues to be built today
Protection	Few protected by law	Proportionately more protected

Characteristics of vernacular buildings contrasted with formal buildings

Thatched farmyard at Ballyduff South, near Ballinagar

nology and land management emphasises the non-industrial nature of the vernacular. Traditional crafts such as thatching, clay-wall building, use of lime-plaster and lime-wash are all supported by the conservation of the vernacular building stock and they provide very direct links with our past.

It may be noticed that many vernacular houses are sited at an angle to the public road or may occasionally have their back to it. In the latter case, there may be no openings in the road wall, usually because this wall faces north and too much heat would be lost. This characteristic modesty is often what gives vernacular buildings their charm in the landscape. They are structures built without pretension. Their usefulness to the builder was the guiding principle and what are seen as their aesthetic qualities today were perhaps unintentional. However, the survival of ancient and/or archaic materials, small openings and simple coloured rendering, has attracted the lens of the photographer to an extraordinary extent.

Vernacular architecture is not confined to the countryside, although it would be true to say that the vast majority of vernacular buildings today are to be found outside towns. The degree of change in towns has usually been greater than in the countryside. Local authorities everywhere have overseen the removal of small town houses, from about the 1930s onwards, seeing them as unfit and unsanitary. Until the middle of the twentieth century, significant rows of thatched houses were to be found in Offaly's towns and villages. The loss of such buildings was only outstripped by that of the Great Famine a century earlier.

References
1. Danaher, Kevin. *Ireland's Vernacular Architecture.* Cork (Mercier Press) 1975, p. 5. Re-issued by Bord Fáilte in colour as *Ireland's Traditional Houses* (1991).
2. International Commission on Monuments and Sites, UNESCO. *Charter on the Built Vernacular Heritage.* Mexico 1999. www.icomos.com
3. Mulhausen, Ludwig. 'Contributions to the study of the tangible material culture of the Gaoltacht', *Journal of the Cork Historical and Archaeological Society,* 38 (1933), pp. 67–71 and 39 (1934), pp. 41–51.
4. Gailey, Alan. *Rural Houses of the North of Ireland.* Edinburgh (John Donald) 1984.
5. Rudofsky, Bernard. *Architecture without Architects.* Albuquerque (University of New Mexico Press) 1964.
6. Shaffrey, Patrick and Maura. *Irish Countryside Buildings.* Dublin (O'Brien Press) 1985, pp. 66–7.

2

THE THATCHED ROOF

The thatched roof is both a masterpiece of technical ability and a feat of artistic skill, and the rural thatcher is a craftsman in the truest sense of the word, embodying those personal skills and values which are becoming increasingly rare in a world in which standardisation and mechanisation are the accepted norms, both in life and in work.[1]

Thatch

Thatch comprises any vegetable material used as a roof covering. It is used throughout the world. In fact, thatch is probably the most-used building component on the planet, followed by clay as the most common walling material. In Ireland today, thatch is usually straw (various species) or reed. Material was not normally grown specifically for thatching but rather as a by-product of other agricultural uses. As it was widespread, it was cheap or free – the straw could also be used for animal bedding and a whole

Thatched roof at Killaghintober, near Ballycumber

range of items, such as seating, matting, even children's toys. The use of the straw for thatching would have been a major beneficial use of what was of secondary importance to the food value of the crop.

'Warm in winter and cool in summer'

This oft-quoted phrase extolling the virtues of a thatched roof, repeated by many owners in Offaly, is a common sense observation borne out by the scientific evidence. The thermal qualities of the material result in very energy-efficient roofs. It has been estimated that 300mm (1ft) of thatch material with a fire-resistant layer beneath and plasterboard ceiling has half the 'U-value' (the amount of heat per unit area which passes through the roof, external walls and ground floor) of a modern slate or tile roof.[2] Thatch is thus twice as energy-efficient as slate or tile and essentially maintains an even temperature through the year. Research done in England showed that the temperature through the year under a slated roof varied between 0–23 deg. C (32–72 deg. F) while that for thatch was 8–14 C. (49–58 deg. F).[3] It should also be pointed out that thatch is a good sound insulator, deadening external noise.

Thatch is a product of a relatively non-polluting human activity. The more traditional the growing and harvesting are the more 'green' will be the straw or the reed. Rotten straw or reed from a roof that is being re-thatched is biodegradable, unlike asbestos-cement slates or concrete tiles. There is also the possibility that straw for thatching could be grown on set-aside land, with EU agreement, as it suits the craft for the stalks to be cut when the grain is not ripe. Water reed could be grown on cutaway bog or through careful management of existing reed beds, with consequent benefits for wildlife and nature conservation.

It also seems that thatch may not be as prone to severe damage from wind as might otherwise be thought. In England it was observed during Hurricane Charlie in 1987 that roofs of thatch performed considerably better than other roof coverings.[4]

The nature of thatching

Thatching is a traditional craft, often handed down from father to son or from neighbour to neighbour's son. Thatchers are now rare. This was not the case in former generations when there were enough thatched roofs in any locality to support several thatchers, all with their own slightly varying technique or decorative devices. Today with the massive thinning out of such roofs, thatchers have to travel over wider distances to ply their trade. This movement of thatchers may lead to a merging of regional styles and the disappearance of some.

Owners seldom consult the classified telephone directory when seeking a thatcher. It is not quite the same thing as looking for a mechanic or other tradesman. Owners usually learn about thatchers from other owners, perhaps stopping at a thatched house and enquiring about who did the thatching last, how good the job was, what it cost, how long it took and so on. As is appropriate for a traditional craft, the information conduit is oral. This informality reflects the nature of the craft itself. Thatchers are interesting and they tend to be the subject of documentary programmes more than any other building craftsman or tradesman. Their appearance in the media is usually presented as a triumph in the face of adversity and they are idealised as working in an environment that has seen the loss of so many roofs, some of which the thatcher in question had thatched himself at some stage.

There are no standard specifications for thatching work. It might be difficult to attempt to develop such a standard, as the craft could be completely undermined if rigid national criteria were to be brought in. At the very least some of the materials in common use would disappear, as would some of the techniques. A national standard would of course have to strive for considerably greater longevity for thatch, but this could hamper efforts to conserve and protect the most interesting roofs which are often very rough. Another issue is the non-standard nature of the building components whose production is variable depending on time of year and the weather, the threshing process and many other factors. Concrete blocks and bundles of thatch are as different as chalk and cheese. However, the understandable demand on the part of owners for longer life for thatching will inevitably lead to the concentration of thatch into two or three materials and a similar number of techniques associated with these materials.

It is probable that some thatched roofs have disappeared because their owners had con-

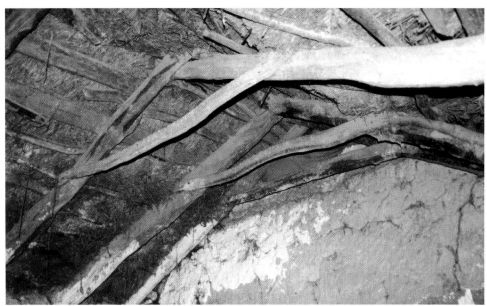

Interior of a thatched roof at Ballyduff South, near Ballinagar

tinual difficulties getting the services of a thatcher. Most thatchers working in Ireland have learned the craft from family members or as apprentices to others. In the 1980s AnCO, predecessor of FÁS, the state training body, operated a course in Galway teaching water reed thatching. In the 1990s, there was a training course of 86 weeks with certification by City and Guilds and run by FÁS in conjunction with an English thatcher, the late Peter Brockett, at Tagoat, Co. Wexford, where thatchers have been taught how to apply 'wheat reed (straw)' using the English 'long straw' technique. There was a huge level of interest, with 400 applying for the 14 places on offer. The advantage of recognised training courses is that there are objective standards and depending on the nature and depth of the training, different qualities of thatching may result. As the nature of thatching is rooted in craft rather than industry it may be more appropriate to see thatchers trained in the more traditional manner, by way of apprenticeship to well-regarded local thatchers. State acceptance for grant aid purposes could be facilitated by requiring the teaching thatcher to furnish references from a number of owners he has worked for over the previous year or two. There is a distinction to be drawn between those thatchers who concentrate on older buildings and those involved with new-build, the latter usually employing water reed.

Traditionally the thatcher would have the assistance of the house owner or an apprentice. Such a helper was needed to pull straw and fork up the bundles to the thatcher who spent his time on the ladder. If the thatcher had to climb up and down the ladder to fetch these materials, the job would take considerably longer. There was also the issue of increased movement on the ladder unnecessarily disturbing the roof.

The thatching season
In Offaly scolloped straw thatching by part-time thatchers who are also farmers has traditionally being carried out between October and February. The start of their season coincides with the cereal harvest and the appropriate time for cutting scollops. Thrust thatch can have a longer season, as it does not rely on the availability of scollops. Full-time straw and reed thatchers work throughout the year. Irish water reed is harvested in winter although imported reed and straw are available throughout the year.

Surveys of thatch in Ireland[5]
There is no agreed figure for the number of thatched buildings in Ireland. However, the author estimates that there are probably some 2,500 in the Republic with another 150–200 in Northern Ireland. There are likely to be about five to ten times as many thatched roofs covered by corrugated iron.

In the late 1980s and early 1990s, Michael Higginbotham of the Office of Public Works carried out rapid surveys of the thatched buildings in seven Leinster counties, excluding Offaly. He later added Kilkenny and Limerick, the locations of the thatched buildings of which had been established already. In early 2002, Mary Sleeman and others carried out a survey of the thatched buildings in Co. Cork. The Offaly survey brings the national coverage up to eleven counties and it is the most up to date. At the time of writing, a survey of the thatched buildings of Co. Sligo was underway. All surveys of thatched roofs are snapshots in time as in a few years time a significant loss might well be noticed in the number of surviving thatched roofs and periodic re-surveys will be vital to monitor the condition of our stock of thatched buildings.

The Historic Thatch (Ireland) Study was a joint north-south venture, backed by European Union funding. It looked at historic thatching materials in all thirty-two counties with a view to growing successful old varieties of thatching materials.[6] Recently the state sponsored a more focused study of thatching and how best to chart a course for the future of thatching in Ireland. Both of these reports are eagerly awaited.

Thatching materials
The Heritage Council advocates that

> Every effort should be made to ensure that roofs are re-thatched using their traditional materials
> ... Reed is an acceptable material on new roofs where there is no tradition, and on existing roofs
> in the short term where there is no other available material. Its application should not result in
> irreversible alterations, for example, to the underlying existing thatch or roof structure and plan-
> ners and county councils should stipulate the use of like with like ...[7]

Traditionally, the materials used would have been whatever could be sourced locally; to buy
in straw or reed over any distance would have involved extra expense. The verdict as to which
material is or was best very much depends on who one is speaking to, whether grower, thatcher
or owner. There appears to be a high degree of subjectivity and personal preference as distinct
from criteria that have been proved scientifically or agreed upon as having the best qualities
for thatching.

Recorded oral tradition suggests that wheat was most favoured and had the longest life.
Against this, it is very common to find individuals who prefer the colour and length of oaten
straw. Caoimhín Ó Danachair found the following to be the situation at the end of 1945, before farm mechanisation and intensification became universal:

> Wheat straw is the most popular in most parts of the country. In Derry, Donegal and Fermanagh
> flax is preferred ... In many counties rye straw comes second to wheat, and some thatchers re-
> commend that a special crop of rye be grown for thatching ... Oats straw is fairly popular too, and
> takes pride of place over wheat in Counties Kildare, Louth, Leix, Offaly and Westmeath, and rivals
> wheat in Meath. It will be noted that all these Leinster counties adjoin. Barley straw is used very
> rarely ... In some counties where reed grows in lakes and rivers, it is used in preference to other
> materials. This is the case in particular in Limerick, Kerry and Clare and to a lesser extent in Cork,
> Tipperary and Waterford – the six counties of Munster. It is rarely used elsewhere. In mountainous
> districts, especially in Donegal, Mayo, Galway and Kerry, rushes and certain tough grasses are often
> used ... Heather is occasionally used on outhouses, while a few correspondents tell us of the former
> use of potato-stalks and such rubbish by unfortunates who could provide nothing better.[8]

In Ulster oats was generally in use but was seen as soft, easily broken and not long lasting. In
certain parts of Ireland flax or rye were preferred and are or have been grown for thatching
purposes. Rye was preferred and grown for thatching, having a strong, but wiry stalk. However, flax was accepted as best of all, but only grown for thatching in years when prices were
very low.[9] Thatchers who use oaten straw are always very enthusiastic about it, preferring it
to wheat. Closer examination of apparently oat-straw roofs often reveals underlayers of wheaten
straw. This shift from wheat to oats throughout Ireland has occurred over the last 50 years.
Barley is universally seen as an inferior material for thatching.

The application of nitrates directly to the field in the case of straw or indirectly as run-
off from fields to which there has been a heavy application of nitrate fertiliser has led to straw
and reed which are prone to premature decay. 'Poor quality material will lead to a shortened
life for the roof overall. Take a bundle and see what falls out of it, if it is bruised with broken
stems, has it been poorly threshed?'[10] This caution similarly applies to reed – if cut out of its
season.

Topographical siting is important for the life of a thatched roof. Perhaps ironically, the
roofs of those buildings which have been constructed in a low-lying position or sheltered by
trees or buildings, will take longer to dry out than those that are sited in a more airy spot.

Oaten straw
The results of the various surveys done for eleven counties show that oaten straw covers just

over half of all the thatched buildings in those counties. Its prevalence in Offaly, at 80%, is far higher than the national average. The surveys on which the figures below are based were mainly conducted in the late 1980s. It is certain that the numbers of thatched and in particular, straw-covered buildings now surviving in the various counties has greatly diminished. For example, the total of seventy in Fingal in 1987 is now forty.

Oaten straw is traditionally harvested by reaper binder in July and August. It is usual for the cereal to be cut 'rare' or about a week before it is fully ripe. The straw is gathered into stooks and left for one to two weeks to ripen. It is then gathered in large ricks, covered over and protected until ready to go through the combine machine. If properly stooked oaten straw will stay good for many months.

At present, it is not unusual for round bale straw to be used in thatching. Such straw is not ideal as it may be over-threshed, too short, have a high nitrate content and may only last two or three years. The opposite is organically grown wheat reed that, if harvested in the traditional way and applied to the roof by a diligent thatcher, should last at least 15 years.

Other cereals
Often oaten straw is only the outermost layer on a roof. Many thatches are composed of more than one material, wheat often being found in lower layers. Other cereal straws and/or materials such as rushes or bracken can be found in roofs, sometimes plugging holes, or in the case of outbuildings, sometimes forming the main thatch.

Wheat appears to be little used today. It was the dominant material throughout Ireland in the 1950s. As the main cereal in production it has long ago succumbed to selective breeding practices and is now confined to a very few highly developed high-yield varieties. It was traditionally regarded as probably the best all-round straw for thatching. It was widely grown as a food crop and its life compared well with flax and rye. It was popular with thatchers because it grew to a uniform length, had the cleanest stalk and needed less preparation than other straws.

'Wheat reed' has been occasionally used by some of the younger thatchers trained at Tagoat in Co. Wexford by the late Peter Brockett. The material is wheat straw that has been passed through a comber, a machine for cleaning and straightening the straw stalks. It is bundled with all heads at one end and all butts at the other. It is so named because it looks very similar to reed in the manner of its laying. It is applied in a thicker coat than is usual for oats, for example, and takes up to twice as long to thatch and is correspondingly more expensive. Most 'wheat reed' appears to be imported from Britain. It is claimed that a 'wheat reed' roof will last up to 25 years, which is at least three times that achieved by oaten straw at present and comparable to water reed. It is still early days for confirming or disproving this claim.

Barley is a material that was usually regarded as inferior to other straws. Rye is commonly used on the Aran Islands where it has traditionally been grown for thatching purposes. It has also been grown for thatching in Donegal and some other parts of Ulster. Flax is best known in Ulster counties. Marram grass is found as a roof covering in parts of Co. Donegal.

The challenge for the growers, harvesters and thatchers of straw is to change the present relatively poor image of straw thatching. If the challenge is not met successfully, we will pro-

Oats	559	(56%)	
Water Reed	384	(39%)	
Barley	28	(3%)	
Wheat	16	(1%)	
Rye	4	(<1%)	(plus the Aran Islands)
Other	3	(<1%)	

Thatching materials in Counties Carlow, Cork, Dublin, Kildare, Kilkenny, Limerick, Louth, Meath, Offaly, Wexford, and Wicklow. The figures are for 994 buildings.[11]

bably lose our straw roofs to reed or to other, manufactured, materials such as artificial slate or tile.

Water reed

Reed is harvested for thatching purposes in some lakes and river estuaries. The extent of harvestable native reed beds is unclear and probably greatly under-used when one considers the amount of material imported from other countries. A number of houses along the Shannon Estuary, north Clare, south Galway, Waterford and on the southern shores of Lough Neagh are roofed in water reed. The beds are rented out and the reed is cut between January and March, by hand or more usually, using mechanical reed harvesters. The best reed grows in about 15cm (6in) of non-stagnant, phosphate- and nitrate-free water. The beds need to be harvested annually in order to maintain quality. Reed that is cut later in the year tends to be very brittle and unsuitable for thatching. An acre of reed bed yields some 250 bundles, six to eight acres being required for the average roof. The River Shannon callows and other wetlands in Offaly are populated by water reed that might be suitable for harvesting for thatching purposes. This could be Offaly's contribution to the replacement of imported reed by native reed.

While reed has advantages, such as generally greater longevity, it does tend to be more expensive than straw but its labour costs are often cheaper. If it is used on buildings formerly thatched in straw, it can undermine the economic basis for straw thatching. Many owners of straw-thatched houses do not favour the greyish colour of reed. Straw thatchers are not enthusiastic about the material either. There is also the tendency for reed roofs to have detailing which is not native, such as raised ridges and details at chimneys. The wetter Irish climate means that the claimed lifespan for reed may be exaggerated.

Reed imported from Turkey, Hungary, France and England is specially grown and harvested for thatching and is used throughout Britain and Ireland. The reeds are strong and hard and when well thatched form a very good and sound roof.

Newly built thatched houses and public houses are almost invariably covered in reed. It is widely seen as having a higher status and the possibility of lasting much longer than the straw.

Switching from straw to reed normally involves removing all of the straw and scraw as reed is usually fixed directly to roof timbers. It might also mean radically repairing, altering or replacing altogether the underlying roof structure. It should be borne in mind that the dense network of branches or ribs and scraw under-thatch act jointly to hold the roof together, having settled into shape over a great many years and perhaps centuries. It may also be the case that thatchers in reed might only guarantee their work if they know the nature of the underlying structure as this can only be ascertained through the removal of the roof covering.

Lifespan of thatch

The performance of thatch depends on many factors, such as roof shape and design, pitch of roof, position geographically and topographically, the quality of material and the expertise of the thatcher.[12]

... it's a bothersome roof – ye're niver done mendin' an' patchin' at it.[13]

Simple roof designs lead to fewer problems than complicated ones with valleys and dormers or flat roofs awkwardly abutting thatch. Orientation is important. A building which has been sited with a gable (often thicker than the other walls) facing into the prevailing wind should withstand storms better than those which present a whole side of the building in that direction. Lifespan is also determined to some degree by the nitrate content of the field or reed bed, the amount of pollution affecting the material before cutting. How the material is stored, the degree of compaction in storage or in transit, as well as the effects of moisture between harvest and thatching can also be factors.

The following sections should flesh out the various aspects of thatch performance, a matter that is of the utmost importance in the whole debate about the survival of the thatched roof. Various writers have noted the expected, but not always substantiated, lifespan of the various materials.[14] A summary of this is presented below.

Expected lifespan of thatching material

Material	Years
Rushes	3–5
Marram grass	3–5
Barley	5–7
Oats	5–10
Rye	8–12
Wheat	8–12
Flax	15–25
Wheat 'reed' (imported)	15–25
Water reed (Irish)	15–25
Water reed (imported)	20–40 (?)

From the above it is obvious that the most commonly used thatching material in Ireland, oaten straw, is towards the bottom of the league in terms of longevity and that imported reed has by far the greatest lifespan.

The three main materials used in England are water reed (50–80 years), combed wheat reed (30–40 years) and long straw – uncombed wheat reed with heads and butts mixed (10–15 years). The lifespan of these materials varies hugely between the south-eastern counties and the north-western, as is the case in Ireland where the greater rainfall inevitably accelerates the decay of thatch. In Offaly, an oaten straw roof near Ballinagar was last thatched in 1989 and a Shannon reed roof near Ballycumber was done in 1978. The former needs urgent work and the latter may hold for several more years yet.

Harvesting and threshing the straw

Sickles and reaping hooks have been used in Ireland since the prehistoric period. The scythe that enabled larger swathes to be cut faster was introduced during medieval times. The reaping machine, which appeared in the 1860s, revolutionised the cereal harvest from the middle and especially the latter half of the nineteenth century and gradually displaced the hand implements. The reaping machine was succeeded by the reaper-binder, which in addition to cutting the stalks also tied them in regular bundles. The bundles of cut cereal were then brought to the threshing machine, untied and fed through. The modern combine harvester made all earlier methods of threshing obsolete in a very short space of time.

Threshing evolved like harvesting, with a progression from handwork to increasingly time- and labour-saving mechanical operation. The earliest method of threshing is hand-threshing – beating the ears of the stalks against a stone until the grain falls out. This technique keeps the stalks intact and is the ideal if labour-intensive way of producing thatching straw. It is unlikely that much hand-threshing is carried on today.

Another development was the flail – two long sticks bound together at one end with a piece of leather. The method of tying varies from place to place and is an excellent example of how a traditional implement reflects local cultural diversity. The free end of the thinner stick, made of hazel was used as a handle (handstaff) and the free end of the other, of holly

Machine threshing in Offaly
Photograph courtesy of Offaly Historical and Archaeological Society

or blackthorn for hardness, made a striker for threshing the ears. The stalks were placed on a large stone or hard floor and the striker was lashed against the ears until threshed.[15]

Mechanical threshing was introduced in the early nineteenth century and was widespread after 1850. The earlier machines were hand-powered with a crankshaft. Later ones (animal engines) were powered by horse or donkey. Late in the nineteenth century and in use well into the twentieth was the steam 'threshing set' – a big steam engine of metal and wood, fed with coal and belching out clouds of black smoke. This can be seen at any of the popular threshing fairs, Moynalty, Co. Meath being possibly the best known. All of the mechanical threshing machines were fitted with drums inside consisting of rotating bars or beaters and/or short iron pegs to beat the grain out of the stalks. All threshing machines cause some damage to the straw as it is important to ensure that as much grain as possible is taken out of the stalks or the thatched roof will become a welcome feast for birds, rats and mice.

Structure of the thatched roof

Typical roof structures for thatched roofs in Ireland are shown on pp. 16 and 23. The 'collared couple' roof consists of A-frames made of rough timbering, the sloping parts of which are termed 'couple blades'. The feet of the blades are set into the front and back walls of the building just below the tops of the walls. Traditional roofs do not have a wall plate such as would be found in a slated or tiled building. A cross brace ('collar') is fixed about two-thirds the way up the roof. These timbers are often small tree trunks, dowelled together with 'tree nails' or wooden pegs and latterly metal bolts. Light 'ribberies' of small branches are laid over the heavier timbers and tied to them by means of straw rope applied with a thatcher's needle. The thatch material is laid over the ribberies, the lowermost layer, whether turf scraw or a layer of straw being tied to the ribberies. Ruined houses near Belmont have collared couple roofs with roughly debarked split-round wood blades 8cm x 10cm (3in x 4in) at intervals of 1.5m (5ft) crossed at the top to cradle the ridge pole and braced by collars 14cm x 3cm (6in x 1in), ribs of branches or split branches 8–12cm x 2–3cm (3–4in x 1in) at intervals of 25–35cm (10–14in) and with a scraw 2–3cm (1in) thick in strips 75cm (2ft 6in) wide.

A-framed roof structure at Cloncon, near Tullamore

In some parts of Ireland, purlin roofs may be found. They are formed of heavy timbers running parallel to the house walls and set into the gables and cross walls. Lighter timbers or rafters are laid across the purlins. The remainder of the structure is similar to that in the A-frame roofs. A ruined house near Sharavogue has the remains of such a roof, comprising round wood purlins 12cm (5in) thick, one at the ridge and one in the middle of each slope with the ends bedded into the gable and cross wall. Round wood rafters 10–15cm (4–6in) thick are laid across the purlins with branches 2cm (1in) above these, supporting a scraw 3–5cm (1–2in) thick. Curiously, the scraw does not appear to be fixed to the roof timbering.

Components of thatch

Straw rope
Two people were needed for this operation, one man on the roof feeding the needle and rope through the roof to the other man inside the building. Straw rope for sewing was made by feeding loose straw into a rope twister, an implement hooked at one end. Often two- or three-ply rope was used, made by tightly twisting the separate ropes by hand.

Scollops
These are wooden pinnings used to secure thatch to a roof. They are normally slender rods of hazel, willow (sally) or briers from osieries or stands of the relevant species, usually along rivers or from any local area of 'scrub'. The maintenance of osieries is seldom considered in the thatching debate but is crucial to the survival of scolloped thatching as a technique. It is also an area that has major benefits for wildlife and protection of the natural environment. Clearance of scrub and osieries, often by bulldozer, is a serious problem for the scollop thatcher. The scollops are harvested in October into lengths of up to 1.8m (6ft). The rods are cut into lengths of 60cm (2ft) or 90cm (3ft), depending on how they are to be used by the thatcher. They are soaked in water for perhaps a week to make them supple. Each end of the scollop is sharpened to a point with three swift cuts. The thatcher usually does this work but

occasionally owners have the scollops prepared already and this will cut down on the time taken by the thatcher. When applied to a bundle of straw, a scollop is laid horizontally and the ends pushed into the straw. Another scollop, in Offaly, termed a 'cramp' (or two, depending on the thatcher) is tapped with a mallet at or near its middle and twisted by hand into a hairpin shape. Cramps are cut from the thinner top of the rod and used quickly to take advantage of their pliability. If left to dry they will harden and may require steeping for a week or so in water before use. One leg of the hairpin may be 5cm (2in) longer than the other, this part of the scollop being closer to the eaves when pushed into the roof and needs to be longer. Up to 5,000 scollops are used on the average thatched roof, although some thatchers use as few as 500, this economy resulting in a roof with a considerably shorter life. Hazel is the preferred species for scollops, followed by willow and briers.

Scraw or sod under-thatch

If thatching a roof from the start, the thatcher or house owner cuts the scraw from a grassy field or from the top of a bog (this latter appears to have been common in Offaly), to a thickness of about 5–8cm (2–3in), a width of 60–90cm (2–3ft) and lengths 60cm (2ft) longer than each slope of the roof. These scraws, up to 6m (20ft) long, were rolled like a carpet over the roof, grass or heather side up (for a better grip on the straw), the scraws of the windward side of the roof ridge overlapping those on the more sheltered, lea side, to provide a good seal. Two ladders were required for this operation. The scraw was secured to the purlins or ribberies by sewing straw rope through. The scraw provided a base for anchoring the thatch proper and a substantial insulating layer for the house. In some places, the weight of the scraw was regarded as sufficient to fix it to the roof timbering. Moss scraw was said to be the best 'as it never becomes dry or hard'. Otherwise grass sods or scraw were cut from a field where the grass was closely grazed to produce a densely entwined, tough and thick mat of roots. In such cases most of the earth was shaken off.[16] It is important that the scraw on the roof not dry and harden to the extent that repairs with the thatching needle would become problematic. Hence, good ventilation to the roof is important.

Scraw under-thatch at Kilcummin, near Belmont

Bobbins
This is a decorative line ('comb') of straw knots along the ridge of a thatched roof. Its purpose is to protect the ridge from attrition by rain and wind. The thatcher twists a small bundle of straw into a loop and ties it with some of the straw. A straight rod is pushed through the eyes of the bobbins and the trailing ends of the bundles are scolloped into the roof.

Thatching techniques[17]

Preparation of straw for thatching
Before use, straw must be 'pulled' or 'drawn', that is cleaned to remove any short straws, pieces of grass and general grit and dirt. This is quite an onerous and labour-intensive procedure. The straws should then be fairly neat, clean and parallel. The bundles used are normally about 90cm (3ft) long, this being comfortable for the thatcher, in terms of bulk and the area that can reasonably be covered within reach of the ladder. Any longer and there would be the danger of the bundles becoming unhinged by the wind. Any shorter, the job of thatching would take longer and perhaps be an inefficient use of what is a relatively scarce material. The straw for thrust thatch needs further special preparation before it can be used. It is steeped in water and laid flat under heavy weights such as old railway sleepers for a week or two. They will still be damp, providing a degree of adhesion to the bundles as they are being laid on the roof.

Scolloped thatch
Scolloped thatching is the most widespread method used in Ireland. When thatching a roof for the first time, the first layer of straw was either pinned directly into the scraws with scollops or tied through the scraws with a thatching needle and straw rope. The thatcher starts at one side of the roof, moving from right to left and working from eaves to ridge in strips ('strokes') about 60cm (2ft) wide or as wide as is safe without moving the ladder. He then thatches the other side and after that the hips, if the building is hipped. He takes a bundle of straw, lays it on the roof, ear end up and cut end down. He secures this bundle to the roof by laying a straight scollop across it. This scollop is in turn secured by two or perhaps three scollops bent tightly into a hairpin shape and pushed into the scraw, gripping the straight scollop. They are pushed in upwards at an angle so as not to trap rainwater that could travel along the scollop and down into the building. When tapped into the roof, the ends of the scollops spring outwards within the scraw, thus tightly gripping the bundle of straw and the spar. The next bundle is similarly laid, above the first bundle and covering its scollops. The lines will be horizontal through the roof, although some thatchers have favoured staggering the lines. Usually a depth of thatch 10–15cm (4–in) thick is applied. At the ridge, the bundles are folded over and scolloped in at each side. The ragged ends of the bundles are trimmed, as the work proceeds, with a knife (an implement about 30cm (1ft) long with a wooden handle and a blade). The straw at the eaves will have a ragged appearance until trimmed with a shears. There is usually an 'overhang' of 60cm (2ft) from the edge of the wall to the outer edge of the thatch. This is important as thatched buildings do not have gutters and a good overhang protects the walls from the worst of the weather. The ridge and eaves bundles are secured with horizontal scollops which remain visible and can be worked into patterns of lozenges or chevrons, or simply lines of scollops (which is more usual in Offaly). The ends of the gable roof require particular attention, as such places are prone to rotting unless protected. In ruined houses, a characteristic setback in the masonry can be seen. Usually the ends of the ribs rested on this setback. The roof was thatched right into the corner of the masonry and a coping added over a few inches of it. This coping could be of clay or concrete and added both to protect the thatch as it joins with the masonry and to secure it further at this point.

Both the horizontal and hairpin scollops are showing in this decaying scolloped thatch roof at Ballinagar

The ridge, in Offaly and some other places, is formed from a rod with bundles of straw looped and knotted around it. The ends of the bundles are scolloped into the roof and the result is a rope effect along the ridge. A decorative 'finial' of straw at each end supplies a finishing touch. Occasionally a thatcher will employ some other device – a Meath thatcher uses a straw pheasant as his trademark. Some thatchers use plastic electrical conduit to further secure the thatch at the eaves, hips and chimneys, but mainly for decorative effect. This is not ideal, as rainwater, leaves and other matter may lodge at these places.

When finished, the roof is given an application of copper sulphate ('bluestone'). This is bought as a solid mass. A good handful-sized lump of it is dropped into a bucket of water, then stirred and sprayed liberally over the roof, about 12.5kg (2 stone) being required for the average house. This is preferably done on a drizzly day, as the thatch is said to absorb the bluestone more readily and it suits the thatcher who might not carry out other thatching work on such

Plastic conduit on house at Coolcor, near Rhode

Reed roof with 'blocked' ridge at Garrymona, Walsh Island

days. The annual application of bluestone is a good opportunity to have any rotten straw raked off and filling and patching done.

Often the roof is covered over with a wire mesh or alternatively, just at the eaves (and hips in the case of a hip-roofed building). Usually in Offaly, bull wire is fixed into the eaves, a foot (30cm) above the edge. Sometimes if a roof is in very bad condition, it is necessary to scollop in a rough initial coat to build up the level of the thatch, having raked off the rotten material. The main coat is then added over this rough coat.

When a roof requires re-thatching, there is often a dipping at the barges. This must be filled first with straw to provide a level surface for the new work. If the eaves needed building up, making a straw 'wall plate' might do. This involved getting two handfuls of straw, twisting them in the middle, folding the lot over into a U-shape and laying it flat on the top of the wall, the curved part of the 'U' facing outwards. The curve was then cut with a knife, thus ensuring that drips would be broken and not run in over or under the 'wall plate'.[18]

It was, and is, often the case that only one side of a roof or perhaps half of a side would be re-thatched, leaving the remainder for another year, especially when there was a shortage of straw. The newly-done part would naturally be somewhat higher than the rest and its edge would have to be ramped as flat as possible to prevent water lodging at this point.

Traditional reed thatching is applied in a similar way to scollop thatching. More modern reed work involves tying the bundles to the roof structure with polypropylene twine. All of it is then secured with 6mm ($\frac{1}{4}$in) diameter mild steel rods (successors to the long horizontal scollops) laid horizontally and fixed to the battens with 22.5cm (9in) steel 'thatching nails'. A legget, which consists of a flat piece of wood with, for example, flattened horseshoe nails driven into it, is used to 'dress' the thatch instead of cutting. Modern reed work almost invariably involves raised scolloped blocking to the ridges and the area around chimneys.

Thrust thatch (see p. 16)
This method is only found in the easternmost parts of Offaly. Elsewhere in Ireland it is used in south-eastern Ulster and in northern and eastern Leinster. In south Leinster, it appears alongside scolloped thatch.

No layer of scraws is used in this style of thatching and in the roofs seen in Offaly or in most of Leinster. Instead, the first layer of straw is tied directly to the roof timbering with straw rope or with tarred twine. The eaves are given a clay topping into which a thick straw rope is secured, the whole way along the eaves, with sharpened wooden pegs. The eaves bundles for the first layer are knotted one-third the way along and pegged through the knot and into the clay behind the rope. The bundles further up the roof are tied to the ribberies. The upper layer of straw is formed of bundles thrust into the first layer. The bundles for this layer are knotted at their ear ends and a thatching fork, a wooden-handled implement about a foot (30cm) long with two metal prongs at the end, catches the knot of the bundle and is used to thrust it into the lower layer of thatch. The under-straw tightly grips the knot of the bundle. The next bundle is thrust in tightly beside the first and thatching continues in a fashion similar to scolloped thatching, although without scollops. However, scollops can be used to hold down bundles of straw required to build up a low spot in a roof. Often, a ridge capping is fashioned from a timber board, a strip of metal or else concrete. The eaves may be finished with scolloping or wire.

It is possible that a closer examination of thatched roofs in Offaly will reveal other techniques of thatching or combinations of the known techniques. This is especially likely in the case of buildings where the thatch is covered with another material. Such roofs may well retain much older thatching traditions, methods and materials.

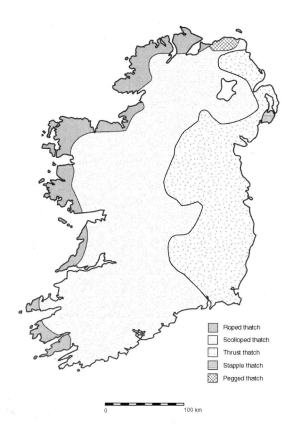

Distribution of thatching techniques in Ireland based on Ó Danachair.[19] Offaly straddles the scolloped thatch and thrust thatch regions.
Drawn by Catherine Martin

Roped thatch
Scolloped thatch
Thrust thatch
Stapple thatch
Pegged thatch

0   100 km

Below: *Thatching terms in Offaly, recorded in 1968–69 by Jim Delaney of the Irish Folklore Commission from William Egan, a thatcher and farmer living at Clonfinlough, Clonmacnoise and then aged 71 years.*[20]

Band	Horizontal *scollop* laid over a *bundle* or bundles of straw. Bands are 45–60cm (1.5–2ft) long if two are being applied across a stroke or 90cm (3ft) if one long band is used.
Bobbin	Twisted straw rope secured to form outer part of ridge.
Bundle	Basic unit of thatch material, 90cm (3ft) long and about 15cm (6in) diameter.
Butt	End of a *bundle* nearest the eaves of the building.
Ciotóg	Left hand. The last *stroke* of thatch must be done with the left hand.
Cramp	*Scollop* bent into hairpin shape and hammered into the thatch to secure a *band*. Two to three cramps are applied to each band. Cramps are 60cm (2ft) long, one leg (that nearest the eaves) being 5cm (2in) shorter than the other.
Comb	A line of *bobbins*, normally twelve across the top of a *stroke*.
Eye	Centre of a *bobbin* through which a long rod is pushed to form the ridge of the building.
Fork	Farmyard implement used to keep *bundles* on the roof before they are put in place.
Hag	Straw or hay rope for securing a bunch of *scollops*.
Handful	Horizontal unit in a *stroke*. There are five *bundles* to a handful, nine handfuls to a stroke.
Length	A *stroke* of thatch. Also known as a 'course' of thatch.
Mallet	Used to drive in cramps.
Rod	A *scollop*. Also the thin pole used to form a *comb of bobbins*.
Scollop	Straight length of hazel, the thickness of a pencil, used as the basic fixing in a scolloped thatch roof. Occasionally sally (willow) is used or perhaps privet. The name 'skiver' has also been used for 'scollop'.
Stitching	Using rope to tie scraw to a roof or to tie ribs to trusses.
Straw rope	When used in building, it refers to a straw or hay rope, either single ply or two ply. Formed using a rope twister or one's thumb, hence thumb rope. Two lengths of rope twisted around each other are said to be 'two-ply'. Also called 'suggan' (from *súgán* = straw rope).
Stroke	Vertical unit of thatching, between eaves and ridge, about 75–90cm (2.5–3ft) wide.

The time taken for thatching a roof varies from thatcher to thatcher. Some thatchers take less than half the time of other thatchers, others use considerably less scollops than others (in one case as little as one-sixth) and the depth of thatch also varies. Thatchers are often very critical of fellow practitioners where they perceive the others' work to be less than best practice!

Thatching tools
All of the tools used by the traditional thatcher are home-made or are typical farm implements borrowed or adapted for use in thatching. The sheep shears, often used for clipping the eaves of a roof, is a typical instance. The mallet for driving in scollops is often made by the thatcher himself to suit his physical characteristics or style of working. The thatcher's rake can simply be a round handle fixed to a flat piece of wood through which is driven a row of 10cm (4in) nails. The length of the rake is up to the thatcher, although many are made of wooden pieces each 30cm (1ft) long. The thatching fork used in thrust thatch is probably the most diverse of the tools used. It can be a cylinder of metal to which half a chain link is welded and with a short handle of wood, perhaps 30cm (1ft) long. In some cases, a more primitive version is a stick or handle with a flattened end, thus explaining the local name 'sticking thatch'. A ladder is an essential item in all thatching jobs.

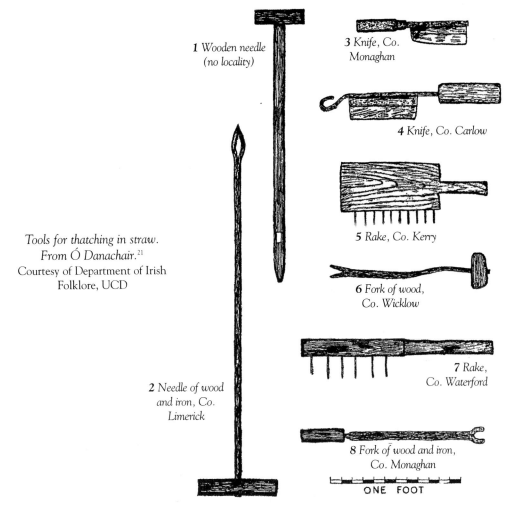

1 Wooden needle (no locality)

3 Knife, Co. Monaghan

4 Knife, Co. Carlow

5 Rake, Co. Kerry

6 Fork of wood, Co. Wicklow

7 Rake, Co. Waterford

8 Fork of wood and iron, Co. Monaghan

2 Needle of wood and iron, Co. Limerick

ONE FOOT

Tools for thatching in straw. From Ó Danachair.[21] Courtesy of Department of Irish Folklore, UCD

Methods not found in Offaly
A variant of thrust thatch is *stapple thatch* in which the thatcher applies a layer of clean, stone-free clay over the first layer of thatch or as bands of clay at particular points such as eaves, mid-roof and ridge as a further fixing for the straw. This method is confined to south-east Down, but layers of clay were also used in Fingal (North County Dublin).

Roped thatch
This method is found along the Atlantic seaboard from Kerry to Down. Straw or marram grass bundles are laid on the roof, but not scolloped in. The whole is secured by means of a network of ropes laid over the thatch to secure it against high winds and gales. Straw rope or slivers of bog fir were the traditional method of tying, replaced latterly by manila rope and more recently, nylon fishing net. The first rope is laid along the eaves and tied to stones or iron pegs protruding from the gables. Further ropes are laid across the roof and again secured to the gables. Vertical ropes are laid from eaves to ridge and over to the back wall and tied in similar fashion to stones or pegs in the long walls. The overall result is a netting of ropes 30–45cm (12–18in) apart.

Pegged thatch
The method is a variation on roped thatch. The bundles are held down by rope, but the rope is secured by hairpin scollops at intervals of 30cm (12in) or by wooden pegs driven into the intersection of crossing ropes. The technique was used on the north coasts of Cos. Antrim and Derry.

Other vernacular roof coverings
While thatch is the 'classic' vernacular roofing material it must not be forgotten that the vast majority of previously thatched buildings now have roofs in other materials. Natural slate was undoubtedly the most favoured and replaced thatch on many buildings from the latter half of the nineteenth century. 'Blue Bangor' from Wales is especially common as well as some Irish slates such as Killaloe and Ahenny. Some vernacular buildings were constructed with slate from the time they were built and these are usually datable to after 1850. Corrugated iron, which overlies thousands of thatched roofs, arrived in the late-nineteenth century, but in its application to vernacular, belongs to generally after 1900. In north Clare, heavy limestone flags were once very common and can still be seen on the roofs of some houses and outbuildings. On the Great Blasket tarred canvas, a by-product of *currach* building, was applied to many roofs in the early-twentieth century.

House with corrugated iron roof at Clonbonniff, Belmont. The visible roof conceals an intact old thatched roof, complete with its original rough timber structure

References

1. Buchanan, Ronald H. 'Thatch and thatching in north-east Ireland', *Gwerin*, 1 (1957), pp. 123–42.

2. Dennison, Gabriel and Ó Floinn, Bairbre (editors). *The Last Straw? A review of the present state of thatch and thatching in Ireland with proposals for the 1990s.* Dublin 1990, p. 7.

3. Fitzsimons, Jack. *Bungalow Bliss.* Seventh edition. Kells 1981, p. 414.

4. www.thatchers.org.

5. Counties Carlow, Dublin, Kildare, Louth, Meath, Wexford and Wicklow; Aalen, F. H. A., Whelan, K. and Stout, M. (editors). *Atlas of the Irish Rural Landscape.* Cork University Press 1997, p. 154 (figure 21); Sleeman, Mary. *The Thatched Houses of County Cork.* Cork 2002.

6. Environment and Heritage Service. *Historic Thatch (Ireland) Study: Interim Report.* Belfast 1997.

7. Heritage Council. *Irish Thatched Roofs Policy Document.* Kilkenny May 2002, p. 14.

8. Ó Danachair, Caoimhín, 'The Questionnaire System: roofs and thatching', *Béaloideas*, 15 (1945), pp. 208–9.

9. Mogey, J. M. 'Thatch', *Ulster Folklife*, 3 (1940), p. 134.

10. Environment Service, Department of the Environment for Northern Ireland. *Technical Note No. 2. Thatch.* Belfast 1994, p. 2.

11. Information from surveys by Mary Sleeman for Co. Cork and by Michael Higginbotham for the other counties; Jimmy Lenihan, thatcher, and John Cronin, Limerick Co. Council, had carried out surveys of Cos. Kilkenny and Limerick, which were then followed up by Michael Higginbotham.

12. www.thatchers.org.

13. Buchanan, *op. cit.*, p. 124, quoting the owner of a thatched house.

14. Ó Danachair, *op. cit.* and Mogey, *op. cit.*

15. Ó Danachair, Caoimhín. 'The flail in Ireland', *Ethnologia Europaea*, 4 (1970), pp. 50–55.

16. Mogey, *op. cit.*, p. 135.

17. Descriptions of thatching methods can be found in Gailey, *op. cit.*, chapter 5; Danaher, Kevin, 'Thatching' in Shaw-Smith, David (editor). *Ireland's Traditional Crafts.* London (Thames and Hudson) 1984, pp. 130–8.

18. Department of Irish Folklore, UCD. IFC Ms 1772, pp. 386–7.

19. Ó Danachair 1945, p. 210, figure 2.

20. Department of Irish Folklore, UCD. IFC Ms 1772, pp. 363–90 and 395–405.

21. Ó Danachair 1945, p. 215, figure 3.

3

THE FORTUNES OF THATCH

The image of thatch

In *Traditional Architecture in Ireland*, Bairbre Ní Fhloinn wrote:

> We must acknowledge the fact that successive generations of Irish people have chosen, and are choosing, to reject the past as represented by the types of houses in which their parents lived. We must acknowledge that the reasons for this rejection are very often to do with factors such as comfort, practicality and expensive maintenance costs. As such, people are not behaving unreasonably in rejecting the old for the new, and the authorities are, to a large extent, simply reflecting the attitude of the community at large to older houses ... This rejection of the old also has importance on deeper levels, touching on our collective psyche and identity, and on the way we regard ourselves.[1]

Jack Fitzsimons, in his very challenging and important book *Bungalow Bashing*, a counter-blast against the proponents of the term 'bungalow blitz', quotes a retired housing inspector who is credited with saying:

> It was not long until our over-zealous environmentalists ... when on holidays in the west of Ireland ... started to bewail the disappearance of our Paul Henry type thatched cottage. What they want to see is a neat little cottage nestling under the blue mountains, without electricity, water or sewerage disposal. Not to live in themselves, you know, just to see.[2]

Fitzsimons himself suggested that

> the simplicity of the thatched cottage did not result from a conscious choice on the part of the originator. It was dictated by force of circumstances – in plain words by poverty. [With indigenous materials] it simply would not be possible to construct a brash building, neither would insensitive siting be achievable. In essence variation was largely a reflection of indigence in different degrees. This included such basics as size of house, composition of walls ... size of windows – if any – and type of roof.[3]

One could question the extent to which vernacular buildings have resulted from the indigence of their owner-builders, as clearly tradition is a major force and one that cannot be dismissed. Fitzsimons also observed the higher status of thatch and thatched buildings in England, which he attributes to a sophisticated long-standing tradition as well as to the adoption of the *cottage orné* (architect-designed thatched house) as an important feature of the English country estate. As a result thatch gained an added respectability by being 'identified with progress and therefore very desirable'.[4]

One could also ask why we haven't developed rural house types to follow in the footsteps of the labourer's cottage. Such cottages were designed and built by the local authorities or the landed estates from the end of the nineteenth century into about the middle of the twentieth and drew their simple form, size and many features from the vernacular housing which it was mainly directed at replacing. The much-maligned bungalow may be a break with earlier traditions, but it satisfies the need of rural dwellers for a roof over their heads and is responsive to contemporary needs and desires.

The challenge for vernacular buildings today is to adapt them to meet modern needs or to identify less-demanding uses for them. Either way economics will dictate that they pay their way or they fade away. Disused thatched (and other vernacular) farmhouses are frequently located in working farmyards with very little ground around them. This makes it very difficult to sell the house on to a new owner (unless that owner is a family member or works on the farm) or to rent.

On the other hand, thatched houses feature prominently in the property press as very desirable places to live. In Offaly, a thatched house with 4.5 acres at Derrinclare, near Shinrone was on the market in 2002 with a selling price of £330,000 and was described in the property press as 'an immaculately refurbished thatched cottage'.[5]

Problems with thatch

Materials

The basic raw materials of thatching have been adversely affected by many of the changes in farming practices. These include intensification of agriculture, use of fertilisers (especially nitrogen) which results in a weaker stalk and reliance on a small number of cereal varieties which give a heavier grain and higher yield, but a shorter straw. Reaping by combine harvester cuts straw too short for thatching purposes. There are only a small number of sources of good thatching straw, often being brought from some distance and thus undermining the traditional local acquisition of thatching materials. Ideally, a number of crops of organically-grown oaten straw for thatching should be grown in each county, perhaps subsidised, at least initially, by the local authority or the state. The straw would have to be cut as low as possible to produce the longest and sturdiest stalk possible. The straw could then be combed in a combing machine to clean it, to separate out long and short straws and to remove the grain. Combing machines also tie the straw into bundles ready for thatching.[6]

Difficulties acquiring suitable thatching material

This appears to be a perennial problem throughout Ireland. While some owners express a reasonable degree of satisfaction in acquiring their thatching material, the question must be asked as to why owners should have to source the material at all. In some instances, the thatcher sources the material himself and thus has control over a vital part of the thatching process and an end result with which he can be happy. Some owners complained about the awkwardness of the enterprise and the unpaid labour involved in sourcing and sharpening scollops and the difficulty in having the straw properly threshed for thatching purposes. A few farmers based in the county or close by in neighbouring counties can do traditional threshing in old threshing machines. With regard to straw, establishing which farmers in or close to the county grow and harvest oats suitable for thatching purposes is an obvious requirement for ensuring the survival of thatch in each county. Reed can be used when it is not possible to get straw, but there is need to be wary about its effect on roof structures and also that it could undermine the viability of straw thatching.

Reed in the southern half of Ireland is mainly sourced around the Shannon but it must be harvested properly and in winter or it will be too brittle and soft for thatching purposes. In general, the reed thatchers are better set up for distribution of their raw material. It should be noted that a considerable amount of the reed used in Ireland is imported from Turkey (in particular), Hungary and other countries.

Difficulties getting a thatcher

A common problem is the synchronisation (or lack of it) between the availability of the thatcher, the supply of materials and application to and clearance from the state for the thatching grant, not to mention the weather. In many cases, waiting long periods for a thatcher has caused owners considerable anxiety. As the winter of 2002 approached, at least two owners were in a near panic. The main practitioner of straw thatch in Offaly, Séamus

Conroy, actually lives in Laois and is in huge demand by owners in both counties. The short supply of straw thatchers is a cause for serious concern. The age of these thatchers and the apparent lack of disciples or successors are likewise reasons to worry.

Thatching costs
It takes about two to three weeks to thatch a typical oaten straw house roof and about six weeks for 'wheat reed'. Larger and two-storey buildings take longer. Ten years ago the average house cost about €3,500–€4,000 to thatch, €3,000 for labour and €500–€1,000 for straw, with a thatching grant of about €2,500, leaving the owner to pay perhaps €1,000–€1,500. In 2003, it cost €7,000–€8,000. The straw costs about €1,000, at up to €500 per ton. Some owners are able to supply their own straw or scollops and this helps to keep costs down. A double ('two-pile') roof or a very long roof will cost double the amount of the average house, say two twenty-two foot trailers of straw. The maximum grant in 2004 is €3,850, leaving, €3,000–€4,000 to be raised by the owner.

The Thatching Grant
The thatching grant scheme was established in 1990 and is operated by the Department of the Environment, Heritage and Local Government and in Gaeltacht areas, An Roinn Gnóthaí Pobail, Tuaithe agus Gaeltachta. The Heritage Council and some local authorities may also grant aid thatched roofs.[7] Its existence is known to the vast majority of owners. The grant is strictly intended for the repair of houses that are occupied full time. It does not apply, for example, to farm buildings or public houses. It is a house repair grant rather than a conservation grant, a fact that has drawn some criticism. At present the normal value of the grant is €3,850. For those owners with a medical card, the grant payable is €6,349. This latter facility is very humane and sensible bearing in mind the age profile of a significant number of owners of thatched houses. The conditions, which must be met before a thatching grant can be paid, are:

> The house must be ten or more years old, must be sound and must be the normal place of residence of the owner.
> The grant will not be paid unless a period of seven years has elapsed since payment of the previous grant.
> The work must not start until after inspection by the department.
> The work must be carried out in accordance with good thatching practice.
> The approved cost must be greater than about €1,300.
> The applicant's tax affairs must be in order.

The department is very specific that the grant cycle not be less than seven years. There is a fear that relaxing this rule could lead to inferior thatching, by introducing the possibility of designed obsolescence that could undermine the whole enterprise. Some thatchers have argued that the interval between grants be much longer, say fifteen years, but that the grant be doubled, to ensure better thatching and the application of thicker coats of better-quality materials. This should result in a longer life for the roof and a less stressful life for the owners and occupants of thatched buildings. An exception to the seven-year rule applies in situations where less than the maximum grant was paid previously, the difference being allowable in a shorter time-scale if the roof needs urgent re-thatching. I have come upon a number of instances where a roof thatched less than seven years previously is now in dire need of repair.

Between 1993 and 2001 an average of seven grants were paid out in Offaly each year. The 35 surviving, viable thatched houses in the county would therefore appear to cost the exchequer about €30,000 per annum.

Insurance

The fire risk for thatched buildings is often exaggerated. While no statistics appear to be available, anecdotal evidence would suggest that the causes of fires in thatched buildings are the same as in other buildings. Arson may be somewhat more prevalent, especially in unoccupied buildings.

As a rule, the thatched buildings in the county, which are insured, are the reed-roofed buildings, owned by young couples with families and public buildings (such as public houses). Most houses owned by elderly bachelors are not insured at all. Two-thirds of the occupied houses appear not to be insured. There is a general perception that the insurance industry does not understand thatch and is satisfied to walk away from providing cover for thatched buildings. I recall a meeting with the Irish Insurance Federation some years ago during which, amongst other erroneous notions, they suggested that the burning of turf (rather than coal) in fires would have to cease in order to reduce the risk of conflagration! The reality is that coal and timber produce much higher flue temperatures than turf and considerably more sparking. The burning of coal in hearths was, at least initially, a *principal cause* of fires in vernacular houses. Sheehy noted in the 1970s that houses with wattle hearth canopies, while theoretically not fire-resistant, nevertheless saw 'remarkably few cases of fire in these cottages over the last hundred years' and she suggested that this was because the vernacular chimney had 'very large volumes of cool air which enters the opening, which when mixed with flue gases reduce the mean temperature down to a pretty low figure and down to atmospheric temperature at the outlet'.[8] Fitzsimons regarded the attitude of the insurance companies to the fire risk presented by thatch as 'archaic, antiquated and unreasonable to a certain extent and certainly, not, as far as can be assessed, based on fact'.[9] This situation has hardly changed in the intervening twenty years and it seems that the same battles need to be fought now as then. Certainly, the insurance industry needs to produce evidence to back its assertions concerning fire risk in thatched properties and embark upon a meaningful dialogue with thatch owners.

Many owners appear to have given up approaching insurance companies at all, having been turned down by most of them or quoted alarmingly high premia. Most of those whose properties are insured reckon they are paying unreasonably high rates. An example is the owner whose average-sized thatched house costs €500 to insure, but whose daughter, living in a much larger, two-storey modern house in the same yard, only has to pay €300.

Thatched buildings can be insured, mainly through Lloyds, which has pan-European coverage. Otherwise, a thatched building will continue to be insured by Irish companies if the building is 'historically' on their books. Few, if any, of the Irish companies will take on a thatched building unless there is a significant other item to be insured – the relatively small number of thatched buildings apparently makes the undertaking a poor prospect. For fire, it would appear that double the standard premium is charged for thatch as against other roof coverings. Clauses that are more restrictive may also be imposed, especially with regard to holiday homes. The insurers regard thatch as a 'non-standard construction', which of course it is today.

The bottom line for many prospective owners of thatched properties is the likely annual cost of maintaining and insuring a thatched roof as against any other sort. If the costs are comparable, assuming that the thatching grant remains in place and that the supply of materials and thatchers is constant, then it is likely that we will retain most of our surviving thatched heritage. If the people of Ireland accept that the retention of our heritage of thatch is important, it is incumbent on us to continue to fund and facilitate traditional thatching.

Lifespan of thatched roofs

Since 1995, at least half of Offaly's thatched buildings have been re-thatched. This means essentially that seven to eight years is the average maximum lifespan at present for a roof of oaten straw before it requires a new coat. Following these trends will be a good indicator of the health of thatch and the quality of materials and thatching technique. Any deterioration in either would have implications for the survival of thatch in Offaly and in Ireland generally. Study of the material gathered by the Irish Folklore Commission in the 1940s suggests that the life cycle of the thatched roof in Offaly has not changed in the intervening decades. One could surmise that either the local climate will not allow a thatched roof to last longer than six or seven years or that thatching in Offaly has always been of relatively modest quality. One observer wrote bluntly that having to re-thatch within a short period of time indicates that 'a) a straw of an inferior quality has been used, i.e., oat straw or b) shoddy workmanship or c) a combination of both, together with other factors'.[10]

How thatched roofs decay

It takes a relatively short time for a roof that needs repair to become a roof beyond repair. There are several observable steps between these two stages. Occupied buildings will suffer this fate if re-thatching is long-fingered (and there may be any number of reasons for this) beyond the endurance of the roof.

Of course, the unoccupied buildings are likely to become ruinous. If left untended, grooving will appear in the middle of the roof, around the base and sides of the chimneys, at the verges (where the thatch meets the gable ends) and at the ridge. Rain will eventually find its way through, trickling through the thatch and down the walls internally and perhaps externally, showing as tar-like stains. At this stage, constant through-put of rain leads to rotting of the thatch over an increasing amount of the roof surface with a resulting cycle of wetting and partial drying of the roof timbering. The roof is on its way to being lost. The eaves' over-hang, essential for protecting the walls, will rot away. Wall tops will lose their integrity and the feet of the roof couples will rot, making the roof structure likely to shift from its bearings and eventually collapse. When part or all of the roof structure collapses, interior furniture and fittings will be damaged. The outer walls will become exposed to ingress of water and tend to come apart, especially in the case of clay-walled buildings. The building eventually becomes a shell with collapsed roof structure in the interior. An 'archaeological stratigraphy' or layering forms, consisting of the main roof timbers lowermost, the ribs above them, then the scraw layer and finally the sodden and decaying remains of the thatch itself lying uppermost. The remains of the roof will over time disappear altogether, if not removed for other purposes. Finally, the only evidence for the building having been thatched at all will be, apart from local knowledge, family memories and perhaps an old photograph, the setback in the gable tops (see p. 58) to accommodate the roof structure for the former thatched roof.

References
1. Ní Fhloinn, Bairbre and Dennison, Gabriel (editors). *Traditional Architecture in Ireland and its role in rural tourism and development*. Dublin 1994, p. 4.
2. Fitzsimons, Jack. *Bungalow Bashing*. Kells 1990, p. 22.
3. *Ibid.*, p. 82.
4. *Ibid.*, p. 84.
5. *Irish Times*. 2/5/2003.
6. O'Neill, Hugh, 'The view from the roof' in Ní Fhloinn and Dennison (editors), *op. cit.*, pp. 28–31.
7. See p. 85 of this book.
8. Sheehy, Margaret, 'Architecture in Offaly', *Journal of the County Kildare Archaeological Society*, 14 (1964–70), pp. 25–6.
9. See Fitzsimons, Jack. *Bungalow Bliss*. Seventh edition. Kells 1981, p. 412.
10. *Idem.*

House at Knocknahorna, near Birr. The roof over two rooms had already collapsed by 2002

House at Cloncon, near Tullamore being re-thatched. It showed all the signs of thatch decay, but now the building is in pristine condition

4

Offaly's Thatched Buildings

The Offaly Thatch Survey 2002

This book follows on from a report written for Offaly County Council.[1] The aims of the survey were to compile an inventory of all thatched buildings in Offaly and to use this information to examine the future for thatch in the county.

Offaly County Council, whose drawing office produced a map in 1990 which showed the thirty-five thatched buildings known to it at the time, provided a head-start for the survey. Amanda Pedlow, the Offaly Heritage Officer, provided more information from correspondence received in response to a request for information.

The survey commenced when all the likely locations of thatched buildings had been marked onto the ordnance survey maps. A few more buildings became known through examining local histories and photographic collections, although these sources were more helpful in relation to buildings that had disappeared or lost their thatch. Altogether 50 buildings were known before the fieldwork started, the figure rising to 82 since.

While the survey concentrated almost exclusively on thatched buildings, that is buildings whose visible roof is thatched, perhaps twenty times the number of thatched roofs are to be found under corrugated iron or other material. Indeed, many such roofs preserve, often more intact, old thatched roofs and timber structures.

Avenue to a thatched house at Derryweelan, Geashill

Some buildings were well known from the outset due to their prominent locations in towns or on main roads or because of their social significance – public houses being a classic example. Naturally, the bulk of buildings were located on smaller roads or at the end of avenues and many of these were brought to my notice by local people, occasionally as a throw-away remark. While I travelled a considerable number of these roads, lanes and avenues, there are undoubtedly a few which have not been visited and which contain thatched buildings or remnants of thatch.

The survey identified two previously unidentified seventeenth-century houses that have or had thatched roofs. Both are two-storeyed; one is roofless and the other retains its scraw under a corrugated iron roof.

During the course of the survey, two of these buildings, the public house (The Ould Thatch) at Cloghan and a brick house near Pollagh were demolished.[2] The latter was, unknown to me, scheduled to be demolished on the day that I arrived to examine it. Thus, my visit to this particular site was opportune. Several buildings that were in poor condition have visibly deteriorated in the space of a few months. Houses at Stonestown, near Cloghan and Ballaghanoher, near Birr fall into this category and demonstrate the merciless effects of the wet Irish climate.

Results of the Survey

The 82 thatched buildings in Offaly comprise 72 traditional plus 10 new-build thatched roofs and is in line with the national average for the survival of thatch. The new buildings and roofs, while interesting as modern structures, have little heritage value and are only mentioned fleetingly in this book, which concentrates on the traditional buildings and their roofs.

There is a very strong clustering of thatch in mid-Offaly, more specifically the area between Ballycumber, Kilcormac, Rahan and Clonbullogue, essentially either side of Tullamore. This amounts to about one-tenth of the county's geographical area, but it contains half of all the thatched buildings. There are somewhat lighter scatters around Cloghan and Birr. The explanation for the overall distribution may lie in the relatively good quality of the land in these areas and an economy that supported a significant measure of tillage. This would have provided a ready supply of oats for horses as beasts of burden with a consequent availability of oaten straw for thatching. There may, however, be much more compelling reasons.

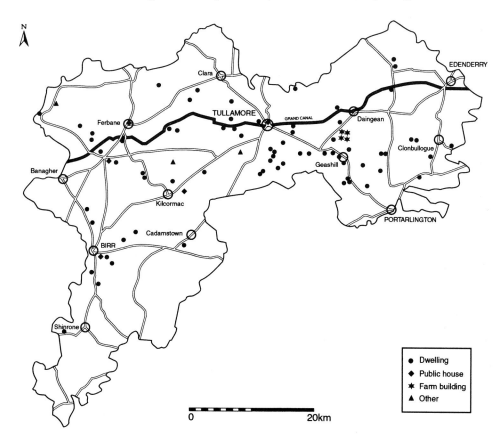

Map showing the distribution and types of thatched buildings in Offaly in 2002
Drawn by Catherine Martin

It is not surprising that the great majority of thatched buildings are dwelling houses. They number nine out of every ten buildings. There are also four public houses surviving (a fifth, at Cloghan was demolished during the course of the survey), four thatched farm buildings, two bird hides and a domestic garage.

The range of building types with thatched roofs was far greater in former times, as noted in the next chapter. There were formerly at least seven more public houses, three schools, several chapels, forges and even a post office. There were of course thousands more dwelling

House in working farmyard at Ballycue, Geashill, happily lived in

houses. Indeed the vast bulk of houses in the countryside and significant numbers in the towns and villages were thatched until late in the nineteenth century. Some such houses are easy to spot, still retaining their thatch under corrugated iron or showing signs that the roof has been raised.

Half of all thatched buildings are located in working farmyards. Another quarter are in old farmyards, one is in a former mill complex and the rest have no outbuildings with the frequent exception of a turf shed. Unoccupied houses in working farmyards are often used as a place to have a cup of tea by the owners/occupiers of the yard. Such houses probably have a bleak future as the owners live elsewhere and are reluctant to sell the house to potential buyers outside the family.

As stated earlier, the vast majority of thatched buildings surviving today are to be found in rural areas. Four of the urban thatches are public houses: The Mallet Tavern in Tullamore, Dan and Molly's in Ballyboy, Hennessy's in Ferbane and The Thatch in Crinkill are possibly the best known thatched buildings in the county. Other buildings in villages are the thatched houses at the edges of Shannonbridge and Geashill. The farm buildings are located near Ballinagar and the bird hides are to be found on Bord na Móna lands at Lough Boora, near Kilcormac and near Clonmacnoise.

Most thatched houses are sited very close to the public road, often with a garden, yard or a slight forecourt between the house and road. Many of these are perpendicular to or at an angle to the road and one has its back wall to the road. In all of these instances, the builder was taking care to orientate the house away from the prevailing winds and a few houses have no windows or doors in their rear, north-facing walls. As with other parts of Ireland, orientation of the dwelling house was taken very seriously in Offaly, two-thirds facing more or less south-east, away from the prevailing wind. Outbuildings shelter a number of houses that face into the prevailing winds. Somewhat less care was taken with farm buildings.

A quarter of all thatched buildings are located at the end of avenues, at distances of up to 1.6km (2 miles) from the public road. Two of these, at Broughal, near Kilcormac, are in a clustering of two farm complexes. It should be noted that in some cases, these avenues may have been public roads in previous centuries, especially when one considers the population and housing density in the mid-nineteenth century.

The arrival of the canal at the end of the eighteenth century must have radically affected the pattern of settlement in the county. The canal only permitted a small number of crossings where previously there had been considerably more. The canal tow paths provided obvious corridors for establishing houses and farmyards, the ready supply of water being a distinct advantage. Some vernacular houses are likely to have been built after the canal.

Scolloped reed house at Derrinduff, Crinkill in excellent condition

Peatland is a distinctive characteristic of much of Offaly. Many houses are located near or actually on the bog. The brick houses at Pollagh are built on peat and the instability of their walls confirms this. In general, the buildings are sited on dry land or on islands close to the edge of the bogs. The importance of turf as a fuel, probably at all times, is seen in the ubiquitous turf shed.

Condition of the buildings
Three in five of the thatched buildings could be described as being in 'good' condition. This term is used advisedly because when deterioration sets in on thatched roofs, they can quickly fall into the category of 'poor'. A few roofs were noted which appeared overdue for re-thatching but which had not actually leaked. On the other hand, several roofs, which appeared as if they would last for another year before needing immediate attention, have shown signs of rapid deterioration, one actually caving in during November 2002. Twelve buildings were in fair condition, eight were poor and in need of urgent re-thatching. Eleven buildings were ruined and two were demolished during the survey.

At Ballyshear, near Clonygowan there is a former corn mill complex. The mill is gone, but parts of the millrace are still to be seen. The miller's house still stands, apparently the survivor of a semi-detached pair of houses. It is a reminder that not all thatched houses were farmhouses.

Dating
It has been assumed that vernacular buildings that survive to be seen today can only have been constructed in the nineteenth century. However, almost all of the buildings are earlier than the first edition of the ordnance survey six-inch maps (1838) and it is highly improbable that more than a few were built between 1800 and 1838. How much earlier than 1800 it is almost impossible to establish. This is true of most vernacular buildings in Ireland. Some of the buildings are likely to date to the seventeenth century, as we know of several early buildings that were definitely thatched. Three houses (at Noggusduff, Gallen, at Kilgortin, Rahan, and at Knockballyboy, Daingean) were probably built after the Grand Canal was constructed in the 1790s as they are close to and parallel to the tow path. We know for certain, however, that the two houses at Pullagh, with walls of the local Pullagh brick, were built between 1838 and 1912 and more particularly after 1850 when brick-making began in the area.

Construction

In his book on the Cadamstown area, Paddy Heaney writes:

> All the material used in the construction of the houses was found locally [i.e., in the Cadamstown district]. The timbers for the roof consisted of ash poles called rafters; the ends were placed on the walls and fastened at the ridge with wooden pegs. Ribberies or scantlings, made from split ash, were fastened lengthways across the rafters. Then the big scraw was placed in layers across the roof and the thatcher took over. The chimney-breast was made from wattles woven together like a basket and covered with marl or yellow clay. The material could withstand the heat and sometimes fire. The local carpenter made the doors and windows. The floor was paved with flagstones with a large flag for the hearthstone, a hob on each side of the fire and an iron crane to carry the pots and kettles. Then the house was complete. The remains of these houses can be seen all over the mountain, and they withstood the great storms of 1839 and 1904 …[3]

The roof

The shape of the roof is a key indicator of the pedigree of vernacular buildings. Pitched roofs, with two sloping sides, are the most common in Offaly – over two-thirds of the total. There are fifteen buildings with hipped roofs, i.e., four slopes. Two of these are half-hipped, where the gable walls are somewhat higher than the side walls and the slopes begin halfway up the roof. Six roofs are pitched at one end and hipped at the other. As with clay-walled buildings, all of the hipped buildings are to be found east of Tullamore.

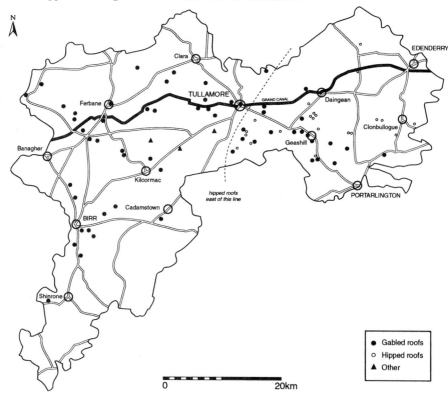

Roof forms in Offaly. Hipped thatched roofs are to be found in eastern Offaly. Interestingly, all verifiably clay-walled buildings are also located to the east of Tullamore. This close relationship may be due to the hipped roof being better able to spread the weight of the roof more evenly over clay walls than would a gabled roof.
Drawn by Catherine Martin

Hipped at one end and gabled at the other. Urney, Clonbullogue

Roof structure
The typical roof structure in the older thatched buildings is made of A-shaped principal rafter trusses ('couples') set at intervals of about 1.5m (5ft). These couples comprise unsawn, roughly hewn timbers or half-round timbers, c. 10cm (4in) diameter and known as 'blades'. The ends of the blades rest in the wall tops and not on a wall plate as one would find along the top of a wall in a slated or tiled roof. The collar beam is pegged or bolted into the blades of the couple about two-thirds the way up the roof. The ridge ends of the blades are pegged into each other or bolted together and are usually crossed to receive a ridgepole. This structure supports a lighter framework of rough branches ('ribs') 8cm x 3cm (3in x 1in) set at intervals of 30cm (12in). In turn, these support a thick scraw or grass sod under-thatch 2–3cm (1in) thick. In many of the roofs looked at, the scraw is not tied to the roof timbers, as the weight of the scraw must have been regarded as enough to hold it to the roof. The thatch itself, in the case of straw, is anchored into this scraw by means of sprung willow rods (scollops). Sawn timbering was occasionally noted, particularly in repair work. For example if it was thought that the main roof structure needed strengthening, an extra one or two sawn couples were added. All of the more recent roof structures are sawn, as are roofs where a straw thatch has been removed and has or is being replaced by a reed thatch.

> Roofing consisted in building rafters, locally called blades or 'couples', which are dowelled or spiked together at the ridge and collar-tied at about two-thirds the height of the roof. Depending on the financial circumstances of the owner, round wood 4" in diameter or roughly wrought 4" x 3" local timber was used with somewhat lighter timber for the collars. All are secured with wooden dowels or spiked with handmade nails. On these rafters laths, known as 'ribs' of various sizes and shapes, from light branches of birch to roughly wrought timber 3" x 1½" are secured by spiking, or by tying with light hempen or straw ropes. On top of these are placed bog rods approx. 1½" thick, these being tied also to the 'ribs' with light cords, or twisted straw ropes. The thatch covering was attached to the rods by tying or with scollops, final coats being scolloped on, the ridge being finished with a capping of pre-fabricated bobbins of twisted straw.[4]

At Ballyatty, Sharavogue, a different type of roof is to be seen in a ruined house. This is a purlin roof, consisting of three round wood timbers 10–15cm (4–6in) in diameter positioned parallel to the long walls, one halfway up each side of the roof and one forming the ridgepole. Across the backs of the purlins are small branches 2cm (1in) in diameter, supporting a scraw 3–5cm (1–2in) thick.

Reed thatching in progress at Kinnitty Castle

A house at Clonlee, Kinnitty, destroyed in a fire in 2000, had a metre of thatch on the roof. The roof structure was 'primitive' according to the owner and consisted of unsplit and unsawn timbers, mortised and pegged together. There was a raft of wattles over timbers supporting the scraw and a thatch of wheaten straw.

Roof covering

Oaten straw is the dominant thatching material in the county, being the roof covering of four in every five buildings. The remaining roofs are water reed and one rye. All of the modern roofs are of reed. Many owners, even of straw-roofed buildings, regard reed as the material of long life. Three of the four surviving public houses are roofed in reed. One of the challenges for the survival of straw in the county is to try to change the perception of the weaknesses of straw. Furthermore, while oaten straw is usually sourced in the county or in neighbouring counties and only occasionally brought in from any great distance, reed is mostly imported from abroad, Turkey in particular. In the latter case, the sourcing of the material runs counter to traditional practice where building materials were obtained locally.

Thatching techniques in Offaly

The technique of scolloped thatching was described in an earlier chapter. Scollops are locally called 'switches' in parts of west Offaly. Many of the Offaly thatches have a decorative course of scollops or even electrical conduit at the ridge and eaves.

> Everything had to be ready for the thatcher. The scollops were cut into two-foot lengths and pointed at each end, the straw or thatch had to be pulled from the reek and placed in rows or bundles. Buckets of water were then thrown on the straw to keep it fresh. A man would be employed full-time to attend the thatcher. A long wooden ladder was required for the thatcher. He first cleaned the old thatch from the roof … the helper then brought the bundles of straw up the ladder. The thatcher had his tools at the ready, a wooden mallet, thatching rake, a bundle of scollops. He then began the thatching process at the bottom and worked up and secured each layer of straw with a long scollop and fastened each end with a key or staple. A staple was made, by laying the scollop across one side of the ladder and hitting it with a mallet a couple of times. Then it was twisted in the weak spot and shaped into a staple. The thatcher had to drive the staple upwards so that the water would not follow it down. When the job was finished a stone or two of bluestone (copper

sulphate) was dissolved in a bucket of water and thrown all over the complete roof. It was then raked down with the thatching rake. The final phase of the job was cutting the eaves. The roof, if sprayed with copper sulphate every year, could last up to ten or fifteen years.[5]

The second technique noted, in the case of four houses in the east of the county (and more widely in the east of Ireland), is thrust thatch. This is known as 'sticking thatch' in this part of Offaly. The implement used is termed a 'spurtle' or 'thatching stick'. A scraw under-thatch seems to be typical in Offaly.

From the Offaly Thatch Survey it is clear that the most common material is oaten straw and the most common technique is scolloped thatch. It should be noted that thrust thatch is employed in some eastern districts. Along the Shannon, new roofs in Shannon reed would not be inappropriate. Imported reed applied to older roofs is not ideal as it flies in the face of the traditional local sourcing of materials. For new or very recent roofs, a case could be made for a more liberal approach.

Ready for thatching. Oaten straw, scollops, rake, fork and ladder, Clogh, Co. Kilkenny

The Irish Folklore Commission circulated questionnaires on traditional roofing and thatch in the early 1940s. Kevin Danaher compiled the information and published a short article in 1945.[6] For Offaly, the picture presented then was that:

In west Offaly hipped roofs were rare and in the east they were dominant.
Scraw under-thatch throughout the county.
Re-thatching carried out about every five years, but sometimes up to seven or eight years.
Mainly professional thatchers carried out thatching.
Scolloped thatch throughout the county although 'stitching' noted on some houses in the NE.[7]

The techniques used for reed observed in the county during the survey involve tying the material with nylon twine to regular sawn timber battens at 30cm centres, similar to those for slate.

Covering in of thatch

It should be remembered that some of the best evidence for thatched roofs and roof structures survives under corrugated roofs. At Kilcormac, there is a pair of single-storey houses with lofts, one is covered in corrugated iron, the other with corrugated felt or building paper, a material which was seen in several other parts of the county. The entire original roof structure survives underneath. Typically, the corrugated roof was fixed to a light sawn timber roof that was nailed or bolted to the old roof structure under the thatch by means of short lengths of timber

Unrendered stone-walled house with owner, Biddy Heyland, at Black Lion, 11 July 1915
Courtesy of Offaly Historical and Archaeological Society

driven through the thatch. As the pitch for corrugated materials, or indeed slate or tile, is usually lower than that for thatch, it is common for the pitch to be lowered by building up the height of the long walls by up to 30cm (12in). Often the junction between the older wall and the additional masonry is visible as an irregular line in the rendering.

One house in Offaly has a reed thatch applied over a roof of asbestos-cement slates. This has apparently resulted in a dramatic reduction of the heating bills. As the building had once been thatched, it could qualify for a grant for re-thatching, but this would require taking off the present roof and thatching again from the timbers. In the meantime, the house has a roof which shouldn't leak, even if the thatch were blown off during a storm!

Walling and other parts of the building

> The neighbours came together and built a house from local material. The stonemason built the walls from stone obtained locally, lime was burned to make mortar, and the carpenter or handyman put on the timber for the roof and made the doors and the windows. The scraws were obtained from the bog and placed on the roof. Then the thatcher came along and thatched the roof with straw. If straw was not available, rushes, which grew a-plenty, were used. An earthen floor was put in where flagstones were not available and thus a new house was erected ...[8]

Mortared stone walls are found in three-fifths of the thatched buildings in the Offaly. Another fifth have clay walls. All of the definite clay-walled buildings are located in the eastern half of the county, specifically from Killeigh to Clonbulloge. Margaret Sheehy observed in the 1960s that a strip along the Shannon 10–15 miles wide appeared to be devoid of clay-walled buildings and that the further east one travelled the more clay buildings were to be found. She went on to write that the clay in question was calcareous marl, locally named 'laclea' which underlies all the bogland and is found in ditches in moorland. The clay was mixed with rushes or rye or oaten straw, water added and the whole pounded into a mortar-like mass by trampling, then cut into blocks and lifted into position on the wall, while still plastic and rammed down. Walls of houses were 60–75cm (2ft–2ft 6in) thick at the base. The clay walls of buildings at Ballyduff South, Ballinagar, are quite thin, at 50–55cm (1ft 6in–1ft 8in) thick. No framework was used. The clay was applied in layers about 45cm (18in) deep. When the walls reached 1.2–1.5m (4–5ft) high the surfaces were dressed inside and out with a spade. The walls were usually battered, more often on the inside than the outside. Window and door openings were shaped with a spade and had lintels of sawn wood or unwrought branches over them. Windows were about 65–70cm (2ft 3in) square and were enlarged from the 1930s onwards.[9]

House at Clonavoe, near Clonbullogue, with inclined ('battered') walls typical of clay-walled buildings

Two buildings are or were of locally-made Pullagh brick.[10] Three others, not houses, have walls of timber posts or re-used railway sleepers with a cladding of timber planks or corrugated iron sheeting.

Mention is made in the Leamanaghan area of the construction of sod houses:

> They used to put up four wooden posts for each corner, and place the other poles across tying them together. Then they would cut scraws in a dry part of the bog and build up a wall between the corner posts. A thatched roof would be put on using birch poles as rafters, and covering them also with scraws, and thatching with rushes or straw.[11]

Sheehy mentions that many houses in Daingean had light loose turf in their partition walls and made reasonably fire-resistant by plastering on both sides. These walls provided sound-proofing and were of negligible cost. She even suggested exploring the possibilities of turf as a building material, especially in the midlands.[12]

Ceilings and floors

The roof of the traditional house did not have a ceiling. From the latter half of the nineteenth century, ideas about hygiene led to ceilings being installed in most of the downstairs rooms in houses. Bedrooms and parlours were enclosed first and the kitchen was the last to be ceilinged, if at all. One reason for this is that the roof space of the kitchen was used as a storage place for horse collars and other farming paraphernalia. Many of the ruinous houses and several occupied, or recently occupied houses, still have kitchens without ceilings. The parlour was given the best treatment, often tongue-and-grooved boarding forming an overall diamond pattern. Flour sacks or the sides of tea crates have also been used.

Flooring was traditionally of trampled earth or mud. In Offaly, pebbly marl was used. Sheehy noted the example of Croghan Chapel, under reconstruction at the time of writing and said that 'the mud floors are very durable and showed little or no wear after 130 years service under nail-boot usage'.[13] Few if any such floors survive today in Offaly, having been replaced by concrete.

Doors and windows

The most traditional door type is the timber battened (board) door, usually of wide planks, with a similar half-door outside – nine examples were noted in the survey. More recent imitations are quite common in the county. Three doors were vertically divided (two of them on public houses). The later timber-panelled doors have in turn been replaced by more recent timber and timber and glazed doors. A quarter of houses have windbreaks, i.e., shallow projections which give a measure of protection to the entrance. Many more have porches added over the last century or so.

Typical sash window
Bracklin Little, near Derrygolan

Battened (board) door with half door
Stonestown, Cloghan

The presence of replacement windows and/or doors often indicates that the house has been modernised internally. The more traditional window type is the timber sash window. It is to be found on almost half of the houses. Pivoted steel windows may also be seen, although replacement timber, uPVC and aluminium windows, while undoubtedly contributing to the comfort of the occupants, have had an impact on the appearance of these historic buildings.

Hearths

Many of the houses have or once had a very large hearth and chimney breast. A heavy timber lintel ('mantle tree', also known as a 'bressamer') spanned the house from the front wall to the back or from the back wall to the end of a 'jamb wall', depending on the type of house. This lintel was positioned 90–110cm (3ft–3ft 6in) out from the chimney wall and on this was built a 'hood' or canopy of wattle construction, tapering on three sides to form the chimney breast. The chimney stack proper begins at about 30cm (1ft) below the underside of the roof. The wattle work is plastered internally and externally. The exposed part of the chimney stack was of stone, light brickwork or wooden boards. Fires were invariably lit on the floor rather than in a raised grate, the latter providing perhaps too much draught. A local flag was used as a hearthstone and fireback (to protect the wall at the back of the hearth). A wooden beam spanning between the lintel and the back wall of the hearth carried a 'crook' (metal apparatus) for hanging pots and kettles over the coals. A wrought-iron crane, also made by the local blacksmith, and with more elaborate hanging arrangements, often replaced the crook. The crane was supported at the top by a strip of shoeing iron spiked to the lintel.[14]

Size and layout of dwelling houses

Their size

Vernacular houses rarely have halls as such. One enters the house directly from the outside. The lobby of a lobby-entry house does not constitute a hall, as it is simply the screening off of a small area of the kitchen. Direct-entry houses do not even have this feature and are more obviously entered directly from outside. Bedrooms or perhaps a bedroom and a

Offaly's smallest thatched house, at Killurin

parlour flank a centrally placed kitchen. In the last hundred years or so, a room flanking the kitchen might be subdivided by a partition running parallel to the axis of the house to provide two bedrooms or a bedroom and a dairy. In such situations, an extra window is provided in the rear wall or gable of the building. Three- and four-room houses are the norm in Offaly, the former making up half of all dwellings.

The longest thatched building in Offaly is the five-bay house at Killeenmore, near Killeigh which is 22.65m (75ft 6in) long. The shortest surviving thatched house is the diminutive two-bay house at Killurin which is 8.75m (29ft 2in) long. The brick house, now demolished, at Turraun was smaller again at only 7.8m (26ft) in length and 3.6m (12ft) in width.

All except two of the thatched buildings are single-storey. Several are lofted, the lofting being fully contained within the roof and lit by a window in the upper part of the wall. The Mallet Tavern on Kilbride Street, Tullamore, is the only vernacular two-storey thatched building surviving in the county (although its roof was raised in recent years) but many more two-storey houses existed. The recent, quirky house near Mount Bolus is of several different heights.

It is well-known that the vast majority of vernacular houses are small when compared to more recent houses. An average thatched house in Offaly is 15.5m (51ft) by 5m (17ft), of which almost two-fifths is taken up by the area of the walls, leaving 50 sqm of accommodation. In contrast, an average modern bungalow is about the same length, say 16m (53ft) by 8.9m (30ft) and the walls account for less than one-fifth of the area. The bungalow has therefore about two and a half times the accommodation of the vernacular house. The challenge is obvious: how to increase the accommodation in the older houses without seriously damaging their character. Chapters 7 and 8 offer some ideas in this regard.

Their layout

Studies of our vernacular houses since the 1930s have shown that the plan of the house, its roof shape and walling materials are inter-linked and form two clearly identifiable combinations.[15] One of these combinations consists of stone walls, pitched roofs and 'direct-entry' plan (see below). The other comprises clay walls, hipped roofs and 'lobby-entry' plan. Curiously, although the distributions of the clay houses and the hipped houses are the same, there is no clear pattern for the lobby-entry plan, which is to be found throughout the county.

Lobby-entry plan

This is a house layout in which a small lobby is formed between the kitchen hearth and the front entrance of the dwelling. A screen (jamb) wall or partition parallel to the long axis of the building separates the hearth fire from the doorway. Doors were traditionally left open during most of the day and a person seated or working at the hearth could see who was entering the house through a small spy window in this wall or partition. This window also provided

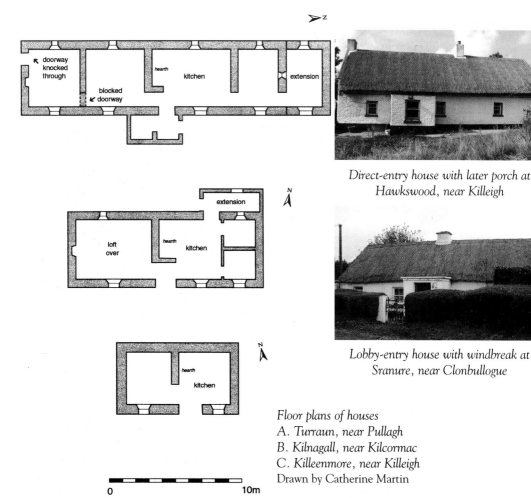

Direct-entry house with later porch at
Hawkswood, near Killeigh

Lobby-entry house with windbreak at
Sranure, near Clonbullogue

Floor plans of houses
A. Turraun, near Pullagh
B. Kilnagall, near Kilcormac
C. Killeenmore, near Killeigh
Drawn by Catherine Martin

some light to the hearth area. The jamb wall protected the fire from draughts from the exterior. Such houses tend to have hipped or half-hipped roofs and clay walls. The latter two features are related as hipped roofs spread the load from the roof structure and covering more equally than gabled roofs. Lobby-entry houses are to be found in much of lowland Ireland, especially the east, south-east and midlands. Twenty-two thatched houses in the county are of lobby-entry plan.

Direct-entry plan
Direct-entry houses are entered directly from the outside. There is almost never a jamb or screen wall and no lobby. Draughts from the exterior would be unlikely to affect the fire as in such houses the front entrance is at the far end of the kitchen from the hearth area. The survey indicates that such plan forms are found (at least in the thatched houses) throughout the county with no obvious geographical bias. Thirty-three of the thatched houses are of direct-entry plan.

Interiors of dwelling houses
Few intact traditional interiors now survive in Offaly (or indeed anywhere in Ireland). The best are actually in buildings that are unoccupied at present or under threat of abandonment or collapse. The kitchen in such houses usually lacks a ceiling, the thatch being visible overhead. Some traditional kitchen furniture and fittings survive in seven of the houses visited

Jamb wall and hearth arrangement in unoccupied house near Ballinagar. Unusually, it has two 'spy' windows

and the hearth is on the floor, under a chimney hood or canopy of brick, wattle or perhaps stone, often closed in with wallpapered boards. The space between the hood and the edge of the mantle piece is a favourite place for tins containing useful household items – tobacco, matches for lighting the fire, receipts, etc. It is also a traditional place for displaying china or chalk dogs or lions and the best ornate jugs. Almost all of the houses, whether intact or not, contain collections of religious pictures, the Sacred Heart being the most common, above the familiar red electrical lamp and often accompanied by a missionary calendar. St Brigid's crosses may also be seen. The most comfortable chairs or armchairs are, naturally, set close to the fire. In one house, the owner was roasting a duck in the traditional manner, in a pot oven buried in the coals of a turf fire. The familiar dresser is present, replete with its collection of plates, jugs, and a myriad of candlesticks, souvenirs and other 'knick-knacks' and sometimes supplemented by a wall-hung 'clevvy' or mug rack. The tops of the dressers are usually nicely carved and represent the only real decoration in many houses. Large wooden cupboards for storing food or perhaps clothes can be seen alongside the dresser in some kitchens. The table, always rectangular, is normally found along a side wall, usually under the window.

Alterations to dwellings over time
Just under half of the houses have twentieth century extensions, grant-aided in the 1960s and 1970s by the local authorities. They usually contain a kitchen and bathroom, although occasionally a combination of bedrooms, kitchen and/or bathroom. Some buildings have extensions that run all, or most, of the length of the rear wall. Many have had porches (usually with flat felt roofs) added. Several houses have been extended in the mid- to late-twentieth century, the new part having concrete walls, modern wide windows and slate or tile roofs. Almost half of the houses have not been extended. A house at Derrybeg, between Tullamore and Killeigh has been extended at the rear to form a square courtyard accessed by traditional-style farm gates. A T-plan house at Ballaghanoher, north of Birr was extended before 1911. A house

Kitchen furniture – dresser, near Belmont

Sacred Heart picture and other items on hearth wall, near Belmont

Ruined kitchen, near Highstreet

at Ballydownan, Geashill was obviously extended in length, the extra bay being slightly set back from the existing front elevation. Two houses have had their plan form altered by the re-positioning of the main entrance. In one, the front entrance, formerly on the farmyard side of the house, was moved to the roadside of the building. In a second, the original doorway has been blocked up externally and accommodates a press on its inner side. Many of the larger houses are likely to have started life as smaller houses. Several houses have had one room sacrificed to provide an outbuilding or workshop and several others have had the reverse process carried out. A few have been shortened through the loss of a room.

Other thatched buildings

The commercial appeal of the thatched roof for owners of public houses is obvious and they are normally well signposted. As profitable enterprises, there would appear to be little difficulty in keeping the thatch in good repair. All of the public houses probably started life as dwelling houses and were urban or village farmyards and have or had outbuildings to their rear. In contrast, the thatched house at Gallen Bridge, near Ferbane was formerly a public house.

Since the loss of The Ould Thatch at Cloghan, Dan and Molly's in the village of Ballyboy is now the only straw-thatched public house in the county, most recently thatched by Séamus Conroy. It is relatively intact, replete with timber sash windows, simple roof-lines and a very wide overhang to the thatch.

The Mallet Tavern in Tullamore may have been built before the fire that devastated Tullamore in

Dan and Molly's public house, Ballyboy

1785.[16] William Garner described it in 1980 as:

> ... E. Molloy's public house. It is a four-bay, two-storey house with lime-rendered walls and a thatched roof, the only example of thatching in the town. The simple shop-front has good sign-writing on the fascia-board and marbled *trompe l'oeil* work on the shop-front.[17]

The building had a straw roof until recent years when the older roof and its structure were removed, the walls raised by about 2m (6ft 6in) and a reed roof added. The square windows on the first floor were enlarged, and the sash windows replaced.

Hennessy's public house in Ferbane was re-roofed in 2002, the earlier oaten straw roof being replaced in reed (front) and slate (rear). This building has a simple, but interesting shop-front. The Thatch at Crinkill has had a large extension, also thatched, added to the rear. This building has the most expansive thatched roof in the county.

Farmyards
Like the rest of the country, Offaly has various farmyard arrangements. Nationally, there are four main vernacular farmyard types and in Offaly, *courtyard* types dominate. These have farm buildings located to the front, the rear (or both) or to one or both sides. Twelve of the yards have houses at right angles to the public road. There are three yards with *linear* arrangements, where the outbuildings are built in line with the dwelling. Only one of the thatched houses in Offaly, at Cloncon, is of *parallel* type, the farm buildings being a range opposite and parallel to the dwelling house. The *scattered* type was not noted during the survey. An interesting phenomenon is the *farm cluster*, a pairing or grouping of farmyards. Four have thatched buildings in the county. Broughal, near Kilcormac is of special interest as it contains two thatched dwellings.

Farm buildings
The range of outbuildings is similar to elsewhere in lowland Ireland. Stables, byres and turf sheds are the typical types. The red ('Dutch') barrel-roofed corrugated iron barn is to be seen in practically every yard and is probably the most common farm building in Ireland. The turf shed is very typical of Offaly and is usually a relatively lightly built structure of timber posts and railway sleepers and with their lean-to roofs and sides clad in corrugated sheeting and timber planking.

Larry and George Hackett's farmyard at Ballyduff South, near Ballinagar, contains no fewer than four thatched farm buildings, one of which was formerly a dwelling house. These appear to be the only surviving thatched farm buildings in Offaly and thus the yard is of considerable importance for vernacular architecture and for social and agricultural history. There are few farmyards anywhere in Ireland with so many thatched buildings. The yard is as significant in heritage terms as any of the great architectural sites in the county. All of the buildings have hipped roofs covered in oaten straw and three of them, a byre, hay shed and hen house (built in two phases), a small shed (formerly a threshing barn) and a hay and general purpose shed (formerly a dwelling house) have clay walls. The fourth building, was erected in 1949 and has timber posts at the corners, clad with corrugated iron and timber planking and is used as a hen house and a general purpose shed.

Several other farmyards had thatched outbuildings until the last five to ten years. These include Killaghintober, near Ballycumber, where a concrete-walled shed built in the 1940s was thatched with scolloped straw fixed into an under-layer of straw, itself tied to the rafters with baling twine. At Clonmore, near Clonbullogue, an outbuilding was thatched until c. 2000. Two former farm buildings have been converted into houses, one at Kinnitty Castle and one near Walsh Island.

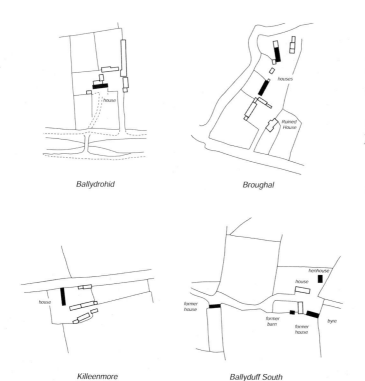

Ballydrohid

Broughal

Killeenmore

Ballyduff South

*Plans of farmyards.
Ballydrohid, near
Tullamore: a large yard
to one side of the house,
with separate avenues
to each. Broughal, near
Kilcormac is a two-farm
cluster. Killeenmore,
near Killeigh: house at
right angles to the road.
Ballyduff South, near
Ballinagar: an
exceptional farmyard
with four thatched
buildings*
Drawn by Catherine
Martin

0

| ■ | Thatched building |
| □ | Other building |

Farmyard at Murragh, near Rahan

Farmyard at Ballydrohid, near Tullamore

Thatched farmyard at Ballyduff South with former threshing barn (left) and multi-purpose building (right)

54

Modern buildings with thatched roofs

Four buildings have been built in the last five years and all are thatched with water reed. Bord na Móna owns two of these, bird hides/interpretative buildings on the wetlands at Lough Boora, north of Kilcormac and at Cloniff, on the road between Shannonbridge and Clonmacnoise. One is octagonal in plan, supported by stout timber posts standing in water and has timber-clad walls, a conical roof and is approached by a short bridge. A house near Blue Ball on the main Kilcormac to Tullamore road, labelled 'Snow White's Cottage' by locals, also features a conical roof. The house is perhaps far removed from the traditional thatched houses, but because of its location and quirkiness, is extremely well known. The other two buildings have more conventional pitched or hipped roofs.

House at Garbally, Idle Corner, near Blue Ball

Bird hide at Lea Beg, Lough Boora

References
1. O'Reilly, Barry. *Thatch in County Offaly: a report for Offaly County Council*. November 2002.
2. I am grateful to Caimin O'Brien for bringing this latter building to my attention.
3. Heaney, Paddy. *At the Foot of Slieve Bloom: history and folklore of Cadamstown*. Kilcormac Historical Society. No date, p. 104.
4. Sheehy, Margaret. 'Architecture in Offaly', *Journal of the County Kildare Archaeological Society*, 14 (1964–70), p. 26.
5. Heaney, *op. cit.*, p. 103.
6. Ó Danachair, Caoimhín. 'The Questionnaire System: roofs and thatching', *Béaloideas*, 15 (1945), pp. 203–17.
7. Department of Irish Folklore, UCD. IFC Ms 1080, pp. 140–50.
8. Heaney, *op. cit.*, p. 191.
9. Sheehy, *op. cit.*, pp. 24–5.
10. A good description of the manufacture of Pullagh brick is to be found in Cloghan History Group, *A History of Cloghan Parish*, 1988, pp. 24–9. The brick-making began in the early 1850s.
11. Leamanaghan Parish Millennium Committee. *A Pilgrim People: stories from Leamanaghan Parish*. 1999, p. 69.
12. Sheehy, *op. cit.*, p. 23.
13. *Ibid.*, p. 26.
14. *Ibid.*, pp. 25–6.
15. Gailey, Alan. *Rural Houses of the North of Ireland*. Edinburgh (John Donald) 1984, chapter 8.
16. Byrne, Michael. *A Walk though Tullamore*. Tullamore (Esker Press) 1980, p. 50.
17. Garner, William. *Tullamore: Architectural Heritage*. Dublin (An Foras Forbartha) 1980, p. 44.

5

THATCH IN OFFALY THROUGH TIME

Offaly's first thatched houses?
In 1990–1991, the Irish Archaeological Wetland Unit, based at University College Dublin, excavated a settlement in the bog at Clonfinlough, 2km east of Clonmacnoise. It comprised three round structures, likely to have been dwelling houses, surrounded by an enclosing palisade of timber posts. They had walls of timber posts and wattle work and most probably supported a roof constructed 'of reed thatch on a framework of light spars ...'[1] The site was dated to c. 900 BC and would undoubtedly represent the earliest evidence for thatched buildings in Offaly.

Seventeenth-century thatched buildings
Apart from the likelihood that some of the county's medieval tower-houses had thatched roofs, the earliest surviving evidence for thatched roofs comes from the smaller seventeenth-century houses.

Hollow House at Ballynasragh (or Tinnycross), north of Tullamore, has attracted a considerable amount of attention over the last three decades. It was built in the first half of the seventeenth-century by the De Renzi family and was only abandoned around 1985. It is now roofless although part of the roof structure still survives. It is a five-bay single-storey house with a lobby-entry plan and a heavy hearth stack. It occupies the north end of a 'bawn' or defensive courtyard with round corner towers. The façade of the house is an eighteenth-century re-modelling. It had been described as 'a very attractive and rare example of a single storey thatched gentleman's house with well finished interiors'.[2] The house has a 'very rare eighteenth-century garden layout with a small lake with two tiny ziggurat islands'.[3]

At Ballynamire, also near Tullamore, Sir Jasper Herbert owned a house of one and a half storeys in 1641. It has projecting end stacks and a central stack with two diagonal chimneys. Evidence for it having been thatched is provided by the rebate in the gable for the timbering associated with such roofs. Lisduff townland, near Kilcolman, has a large six-bay two-storey house that was last thatched about 1920 by Danny Delahunt. It is a roofless shell now and has a return at the rear (possibly for a stairs) and much evidence for the blocking up of some windows and the opening up of others. The house has a very large fireplace at one end and the chimney projects from the gable. At Killeigh, a late-sixteenth/early-seventeenth century house may be the house noted as having a thatched roof and granted to Edward Darcy in 1569.[4]

Reconstruction of Bronze Age houses at Clonfinlough, Co. Offaly, c. 900 BC
Courtesy of Irish Archaeological Wetland Unit, UCD

Hollow House, Tinnycross, near Tullamore, 1978
Courtesy of Irish Architectural Archive

Early house at Ballytoran, Shinrone

There is a large farmhouse at Ballytoran townland, Kilcomin, that is certainly early seventeenth century. It was first noted by Maurice Craig in 1973.[5] It has four bays (and possibly has a blocked fifth bay) and is two-storeyed. It has stout chimney-stacks with diagonally set chimneys typical of the period. It was thatched until recent decades when the straw was removed and the roof covered in corrugated iron but retains a sod under-thatch. It is the most intact early building in the county with surviving evidence of its thatched roof.

Thatched buildings from AD 1700 to yesterday
Mr and Mrs Hall made the following observations about the Bog of Allen in Offaly in 1840:

> ... here and there a cabin rears its roof a few feet away above the surface from which it can scarcely be distinguished. It is hardly possible to imagine more wretched hovels than those which the turf-cutters inhabit ... When settling, his first care is to procure shelter from the wind and rain; he selects, therefore, a dry bank a little beyond the influence of floods; here he digs a pit, for it is nothing more, places at the corners a few sticks of bog-wood, and covers the top with 'flakes' of heath, leaving a small aperture to let out the smoke. Yet the inhabitants of this miserable district, existing in this deplorable manner, are by no means unhealthy, and around their huts we saw some of the finest children we have seen in Ireland.[6]

Such references are frequently the only mentions we have of the housing of the vast bulk of the Irish population in the early nineteenth century. In about 1820, the antiquarian George Petrie sketched a settlement of thatched houses along the roadside at Clonony Castle, near Banagher.[7] The buildings or their foundations are quite possibly those of houses built at the same time as the castle in the sixteenth century.

In *The Miseries and Beauties of Ireland*, published in London in 1837, Jonathan Binns illustrated the cabin, near Daingean, of Barney Mangin, 'the walls of which were cut out of the solid moss ... window or chimney it had none'.[8]

Barney Mangin's cabin, near Daingean, about 1836

Setback in gable giving evidence of former thatched roof. Ballyatty, Sharavogue

We know that few of these very poor dwellings survived the catastrophe of the Great Famine. The numbers of dead or emigrated correspond very closely with the population of what was categorised in official reports as 'Class Four' housing. Undoubtedly traces of some of these dwellings could be discovered by means of archaeological excavation. Although more commodious than any of the dwellings noted by the Halls, the house (now demolished), which stood on the bog at Turraun gave a very rough idea of the cramped housing. This, the smallest house recorded during the survey, was a mere 7.8m (26ft) long by 3.6m (12ft) wide. The height from ground to eaves was 1.8m (6ft). The walls were constructed of local Pollagh bricks and at the time of recording, the walls were starting to burst. The total usable space in this house was only slightly more than that of the average living-room in a modern semi-detached house and, of course, had to accommodate the whole spectrum of activities required for what were much larger families than today's.

While 75 buildings have thatch as their working roof covering, as many as ten or even twenty times this number have a thatched roof under a later corrugated covering. The presence of corrugated iron as a roof covering is a sign of the building having been formerly thatched. These roofs, which were covered as recently as the 1980s or as early as the 1920s, could be re-thatched and in a few case the owners are already thinking along these lines. In the case of ruined buildings, only the setback in the gable walls indicates the former presence of a thatched roof.

While the vast majority of thatched buildings are, and were, single-storeyed, there were a number of two-storeyed until recently. The Mallet Tavern in Tullamore is the only surviving two-storey thatched building in Offaly. There were two-storey public houses in Shinrone and Cloghan. In addition to three seventeenth-century houses there was Cox's two-storey 'thatched mansion' at Ballylevin, near Killeigh that was slated about 1987. The term 'mansion' has often been applied to large two-storey thatched houses.

Schools

At Killurin, there was a mud-walled thatched structure in 1824 in use as a school.[9] Sheehy mentions hedge school buildings in Offaly which were thatched and which had mud walls. They were at Clonbulloge, Clonmore, Killaghy and Raheen. There appears to be no trace of these buildings today. The schools were very small in size, two having dimensions of 6m (20ft) by 3.5m (11–12ft).[10] Broughal School was thatched and survived until about 1928 when it was demolished.[11]

Churches

Lackaroe Chapel, near Cadamstown, was thatched. It was blown down on the Night of the Big Wind, 1 January 1839 and was replaced by the present church in the village in 1842.[12] There was also a thatched chapel at Kinnitty which was rebuilt, slated and glazed in 1830.[13] St Carthage's Church at Killina was formerly a single-cell thatched chapel. By 1817 transepts had been added, a tower was added in 1867, porches added in 1966 and the whole building was clad in artificial stone and given a tiled roof. The thatched roof had been removed long before this.[14]

Public houses

The Beehive at Mount Bolus was photographed around 1901. It was single-storey and also known as Joanna Commons.[15] The thatch was removed, a second storey added and the building altered about 1940. At Shinrone, the Castle Bar, also a dwelling house was destroyed by fire in 1922 and rebuilt with a slate roof, parts of the building were demolished and an extra chimney was added so the building is hardly recognisable today as that pictured around 1900.[16] The Mallet Tavern in Tullamore was raised by about two metres and the older straw roof replaced with reed. Dempsey's in Cadamstown was also a thatched pub, as was the Thatch in Loughroe, near Rahan. Byrne's public house at Clonygowan was also formerly thatched, as was Spain's in Shinrone.

Kilcommon's public house, Cloghan, 1974.
Demolished 2002
Courtesy of Irish Architectural Archive

Other buildings

A charming photograph from about 1910 shows the wedding party of James Kelly and Ellen Daly outside the old thatched post office at Rahan. The postmaster, Arthur Doran, features prominently with his peaked cap.[17] The building is now used as a farm shed and has a corrugated iron barrel roof. It no longer shows any indication of its former status in the community. There were thatched forges at Ballinagar and Cadamstown, their existence belying the dangers of juxtaposing fire with straw. About the roofless shell remains of the latter Paddy Heaney wrote:

Old post office at Rahan
Courtesy of Offaly Historical and
Archaeological Society

> I can still see the inside of the old forge. It had a thatched roof and an old earthen floor with the anvil taking up the centre. The big bellows, the long ash handle with the weight attached, the hood for the fire, the horses' shoes hanging from a rack on the wall, the tools laid out on the bench and of course, the big eight-stone pot full of water. This pot was used to cool the red-hot iron and, most importantly, it was used to cure warts ...[18]

Urban houses

Tullamore had many examples of rows of small thatched houses. Those at Whitehall were demolished in the 1880s and three-bay single-storey houses, which would not have looked very different, were built in their place. These replacement houses were themselves demolished in the 1950s.[19] Clontarf Road appeared in postcards and consisted of rows of three-bay single-storey thatched houses, some already in bad repair in the mid-1940s, when the street was photographed and just a few years before the houses were demolished and replaced by the local authority scheme of two-storey houses standing today.[20] The houses themselves were probably built around the time of the construction of the Grand Canal as the street runs parallel to the canal. Several other streets in the town also had rows of thatched houses.

Elsewhere in the county, Portarlington had similar rows and River Street in Clara had a pair of two-storey thatched houses.[21] One has been raised, slated and the front greatly altered; the other is intact except that the roof is corrugated iron.

Urban houses on Clontarf Road, Tullamore, 1940s
Courtesy of Offaly Historical and Archaeological Society

Rural houses
Countless numbers of thatched houses in Offaly, and indeed elsewhere in Ireland, have been either re-roofed in another material or demolished altogether. Some of them have been photographed and have appeared in the various local histories. Many others survive as memories or old photographs in the possession of the families who live or lived in them. A small few are better known because of their great age or because they have been noted by architectural historians.

Miletree House, Whiteford, Birr was a thatched house with a single-storey symmetrical front and a two-storey rear. In this building, 'all the articles of classical precedent are intact in miniature'.[22] The date of its construction is unknown. It was, however, demolished about 1992. Shepherd's Wood, Tullamore was designed by Michael Scott in 1945 for Desmond Williams of Tullamore Dew, while he was working on Tullamore General Hospital. The house was very cold because a gap for ventilation between the wall tops and the roof was too big. The walls are concrete, with stone-faced chimneys and generally large windows. The roof is partly of sawn rafters, partly railway sleepers, due to shortage of timber during the Emergency. It was thatched with Shannon reeds[23] and in the 1960s, it had a covering of Norfolk reed.[24] The thatch was removed in 1984 and replaced with tile.[25]

At Lavagh, near Lusmagh, the thatch was removed about 1982 and replaced by corrugated felt. In 1997, the scraw was removed and in 1998, corrugated steel was applied. The old roof of bog oak remains.

House at Ballylennon,
Kilclonfert, 1975, now
demolished
Courtesy of Michael
Byrne

References

1. Moloney, Aonghus, Jennings, David, Keane, Margaret and McDermott, Conor. *Irish Archaeological Wetland Unit Transactions Volume 2: Excavations at Clonfinlough, Co. Offaly.* Dublin (UCD) 1993, p. 65. Also reproduced in McDermott, Conor, 'The prehistory of the Offaly peatlands' in Nolan, William and O'Neill, Timothy P. (editors), *Offaly: History and Society.* Dublin (Geography Publications) 1998, p. 17.

2. Knight of Glin, Griffin, David J. and Robinson, Nicholas K. *Vanishing Country Houses of Ireland.* Dublin (Irish Architectural Archive and the Irish Georgian Society) 1988, p. 121.

3. Craig, Maurice. *The Architecture of Ireland.* London (Batsford) 1982, pp. 134, 136 (photograph).

4. O'Brien, Caimin and Sweetman, David. *Archaeological Inventory of County Offaly.* Dublin (Stationery Office) 1997, p. 175.

5. Craig, Maurice. *Preliminary Report of Survey of Areas of Historic and Artistic Interest in County Offaly.* Dublin (An Foras Forbartha) 1973: 'an eighteenth century farmhouse, gable ended with a façade of four bays and two storeys'.

6. Mr and Mrs S. C. Hall. *Ireland: Its scenery, character, etc.* 3 vols London 1841–3. Volume 2, p. 191.

7. Reproduced in Nolan, William and O'Neill, Timothy P. (editors). *Offaly: History and Society.* Dublin (Geography Publications) 1998, p. 438.

8. I am grateful to Michael Byrne, Offaly Historical and Archaeological Society, for this reference.

9. Kearney, John. *Killeigh and Geashill: a pictorial record.* Tullamore (Esker Press) 1990, p. 90.

10. Sheehy, Margaret. 'Architecture in Offaly', *Journal of the County Kildare Archaeological Society*, 14 (1964–70), p. 28.

11. Kilcormac Historical Society. *Kilcormac–Killoughey Parish Album.* Ferbane 1996, p. 41.

12. Heaney, Paddy. *At the Foot of Slieve Bloom: history and folklore of Cadamstown.* Kilcormac Historical Society. No date, *infra.*

13. *Ibid.*, p. 41.

14. Wrafter, Sr Oliver. *Rahan Looks Back.* Rahan 1989, p. 9.

15. Kilcormac Historical Society. *Kilcormac–Killoughey Parish Album.* Ferbane 1996, p. 32. Also reproduced in *Up Killoughey! A history of the G.A.A. 1888–1988*, 1988, p. 11.

16. Mac Mahon, Noel. *In the Shadow of the Fairy Hill: Shinrone and Ballingarry – a history.* Shinrone 1998, p. 98.

17. Wrafter, *op. cit.*, front cover, p. 79.

18. Heaney, *op. cit.*, p. 59.

19. Byrne, Michael. *Tullamore Town Album.* Tullamore (Esker Press) 1988, plate 50.

20. *Ibid.*, plates 70–71.

21. Reproduced in Quinn, D. B. 'Clara: a midland industrial town', in Nolan, William and O'Neill, Timothy P. (editors). *Offaly: History and Society.* Dublin (Geography Publications) 1998, p. 821, plate 23.6.

22. McCullough, Niall and Mulvin, Valerie. *A Lost Tradition: the nature of architecture in Ireland.* Dublin (Gandon Editions) 1987, pp. 45 (drawing), 55, 59 (photograph), 61.

23. Collins, Pan. 'Mist beyond memory', *Creation*, December 1957.

24. Sheehy, *op. cit.*, p. 28.

25. I am grateful to the current owner, Johann Thieme, for this information.

6

Thatchers and Thatch Owners

Thatchers in Offaly

Séamus Conroy
One of the most active thatchers in the county is Séamus Conroy of Clonaslee, Co. Laois, a few miles outside the boundary with Offaly. He is part thatcher, part farmer and is currently training in his son. He works in oaten straw and thatches 5–6 houses per year, between September and June. He was taught by Ted McEvoy at the age of seventeen and started by thatching his own house at Rearybeg, Clonaslee and has been thatching since with the odd break. He works in Laois, Offaly, and parts of Kilkenny, Tipperary and Galway. He has thatched fifteen of Offaly's buildings, mainly between Clara and Clonygowan. He takes about three weeks for the average house, '18 long days', nine for each side of the building. He has thatched one house, at Mountrath, Co. Laois, from scratch. He estimates that his thatched roofs last a good ten years, with bluestone applied every year.

Emmet Dolan
He lives just north of Tullamore. He saw thatching as an unusual profession, did an apprenticeship with the Rural Development Commission in England, and qualified with City and Guilds in 1999 after a two to three course. He has thatched, mainly in reed, but also scolloped rye (at Aghananagh, near Tullamore). Several modern buildings in the mid-Offaly area are his work, including the house at Idle Corner, Blue Ball. He uses Turkish reed, as good quality native reed is difficult to get.

Larry Hackett
Now retired, he thatched extensively until the early 1990s in a ten-mile radius of the farm he and his brother George run at Ballinagar. The farm is notable for its four thatched buildings, the only ones extant in Offaly and they are unlikely to have survived had there not been a

Séamus Conroy at Clogh, Co. Kilkenny

Emmet Dolan at Kinnity Castle

Larry Hackett at his home place

thatcher in the family. Larry has thatched twenty-seven of the buildings that survive today. He learned his craft from Isaac Moore who died about 1950. Larry used to pull the straw for Isaac when the latter, who was in his late seventies at the time, thatched on the Hackett farm. Larry's first attempts were not great but one day, when the master was ill, Larry had to complete the job and did so successfully. Eventually people in the locality realised that he could thatch and his first job was patching Buckley's house at Ballycue, Geashill; later he was asked to thatch the house. Larry does 'sticking thatch', i.e., thrust thatching, although he has also done scolloped thatching. He took about two to three weeks to thatch an average house.

William Egan

A farmer and part-time thatcher, now deceased, he lived at Clonfinlough, near Clonmacnoise. Jim Delaney of the Irish Folklore Commission recorded him in early 1969. When he was thatching his own house in late 1968, he was filmed by the National Museum of Ireland and samples of his work are in the museum's folk-life collection. A list of terms collected from him appears in Chapter 2. He learned his trade by attending his father, also a thatcher. He used to thatch from November onwards, the 'dead' time of the year. He worked in oaten straw, but also on occasion, rye and wheat.

Other thatchers who work or have worked in Offaly

Ben Purcell is well known in the Killeigh area. He thatches his own house on the main Tullamore to Mountmellick road and has thatched many others. *Seán Brennan* from Portlaoise uses electrical conduit at the eaves, hips and chimneys and so his work is quite distinctive. He has thatched several houses in east Offaly. *Ted McEvoy*, also from the Portlaoise area has thatched in Offaly. Kildare thatchers *Christy* and *John Brereton* from Prosperous and *Tom McNally* from near Edenderry, have all worked in thrust thatch in east Offaly. *Jack Higgins*, now retired, from The Pigeons, Co. Roscommon thatched some Offaly houses and was highly regarded.

The reed thatchers tend to be considerably younger than the straw thatchers. They also are listed in the classified telephone directories. The straw thatchers mainly come from Offaly or adjoining counties. All but two of the reed thatchers are from other far-flung counties. *Kyran O'Grady* from Co. Wicklow has thatched two of the county's public houses, The Mallet Tavern in Tullamore and The Thatch at Crinkill. *Brian Rogers* from Co. Sligo thatched Bord na Móna's bird hide at Lough Boora.

The owners

Often a person who could not afford the services of a thatcher would instead try to carry out his own roof repairs. In such cases, the courses or strokes of thatch would reappear very quickly and the roof would start to deteriorate again. Many men who were good thatchers didn't go looking for work, knowing how hard the life was and contented themselves with only doing their own buildings or the odd roofs for others. A considerable numbers of owners would have been capable of thatching their own houses in former times, especially if they were living on the land and growing some cereal crops. Many owners or members of their families have patched and continue to patch their houses and this is an important skill as there can be delays while waiting for a professional thatcher. Timely patching could make a major difference as regards the amount of work needed on a roof.

Professional thatchers would normally receive help from the owner who would attend the thatcher by having pulled the straw and perhaps arranged it into tight bundles ready for thatching. He may also have sharpened the scollops, a time-consuming task which would otherwise add to the thatcher's time at the site.

Age of the occupants

There is a high prevalence of elderly owners of thatched houses in the county and this is reflected throughout Ireland. Bachelors and widowers over the age of 50 years account for one in five owners and elderly unmarried women and widows are one in ten. Half of all the occupied houses are lived in by persons of 60 years of age or older. Young families occupy about one in ten houses, although they have tended to alter the buildings internally or add large extensions.

Bodies such as the local authorities and the health boards have responsibility for contributing to the well-being of the elderly and infirm. They are concerned to ensure that the elderly, in particular, are afforded good housing. In the case of houses of often unrecognised interest or importance, the implications of remedial works on old houses needs to be carefully considered by local authorities and health boards. There have been instances where these organisations have inadvertently undermined the heritage value of such buildings.

The trials and tribulations of the owners and occupants of Offaly's thatched houses, as told to me, have greatly contributed to this book.

Jim and Philomena Tooher,
Ballyegan, Birr

Mary Garahy,
Derrinduff, Crinkill

Kieran Brennan,
Aghanannagh, near Tullamore

7

THE FUTURE

> The bleak and indisputable truth is that the whitewashed farmhouse nestling in to the side of the hill, captured on film on a hot summer's day, is one thing. It is another thing to be the personal guardian of such a building, committed to it for 24 hours a day, 365 days in every year.[1]

It must be emphasised that the future of Offaly's thatch is in the hands of the owners of thatched buildings. No amount of legislation or wishful thinking can keep people living in, and using, thatched buildings. Neighbours, family and friends can, however, encourage owners to retain such buildings. Grant aid and 'listing' by the state and local authorities is a recognition of the cultural importance of thatch as well as a vehicle for providing financial assistance. This book aims to further these goals by helping to place thatch and the thatched buildings in a national and international context. It also suggests ways of protecting such buildings. The key to the future of the buildings is that they continue to be used and occupied while satisfying the needs of their owners.

Guidance for owners
This is an area that has bedevilled vernacular architecture in general and thatch in particular. The following questions should have straightforward, easily accessible answers, but often do not:

What are the appropriate materials for my house?
Where do I get these materials? (You can rule out your local builders' providers!)
How do I go about getting a thatcher?
How much will thatching cost?
Is there any grant assistance?
Is my building 'listed' and is this good or bad?

It is hoped that this book may help fill the information deficit. It should be borne in mind that the situation is not static as grant amounts may change over time and new criteria may be brought in. The issues facing thatch are such that for any approach to be effective and useful, a close eye will have to be kept on the buildings. They should be inspected on at least an annual basis and contact maintained with owners in order for the relevant authorities to respond effectively and in a pro-active way.

Why is thatch important?
In a world that is changing rapidly, it is essential to retain links and continuity with the past with all its lessons for the present and the future. We owe it to past and future generations at least to retain what is good of our heritage. Protecting and maintaining our heritage of thatch enhances local areas in many ways – visually and aesthetically, economically (e.g., helping to sustain a 'green' image for a county or district), socially (providing employment for thatchers and others who might repair and maintain such buildings; improved quality of housing; local pride). It should be remembered that thatched houses that lie disused and which may fall into ruins could be rehabilitated to provide dwellings. Ireland is marketed strongly in terms of tradition and 'traditional' landscapes. It is vital for tourism that we understand and protect the built heritage. A degraded landscape or townscape has little attraction for the tourist, whether he or she is from this country or abroad. Our heritage of vernacular architecture and in

House at Ballyegan, near Birr. Re-thatched in 2002 by Séamus Conroy

particular thatch is an immense resource for teachers and students. Awareness of the natural and built environment requires us all to look for alternatives to what are often very wasteful building practices. An example is the needless demolition and replacement of old buildings. The lessons learned from looking at and experiencing historic buildings, and talking to their occupants, can be a valuable learning opportunity.

Adapting and extending buildings

> Knowledge of the ways of using local materials has gradually declined so that today the owner of a traditional building is looking for a team of rare specialists – to thatch, to slate with local slates, to repair earth walls, to find and use local stone, to make mortars and plasters from lime, and so on. He or she – the owner – will also be paying specialist prices for the privilege.[2]

Working on a historic building can be an ordeal not only for the owner but also for the building itself. The modern building industry is set up for dealing with new structures constructed from mass-produced components, such as concrete blocks and standard timber specifications. It runs into trouble with old buildings that are often irregular and may have no standard components. It might be fair to say that today few builders would have the expertise to adequately tackle historic buildings. There are ways and means of adapting and extending a building without causing distress to the building or harm to its historic character. See Chapter 8 for some tips for avoiding needless problems in such situations.

Rear extensions have been commonplace, especially since the 1960s and resulting from state grants for the provision of bathrooms in houses. These extensions have the added advantage of generally not impinging on the front of the building. The flat roof kitchen and/or bathroom extension may have a limited life and not normally be of any great visual beauty, but it has certainly allowed a huge number of houses to continue to be comfortable for their occupants.

From the conservation standpoint, it is important that the plan or footprint of the original building is still obvious. Thus, extensions that result in a T-plan building rather than an L-plan are preferable. Some houses have extensions along the whole of their rear walls, which have seen rear windows stranded inside the expanded house or blocked up or partly blocked up and used as cupboards. This type of extension is more likely to lead to removal of more of the original rear wall to provide multiple connections between old and new.

Opening up or removal of walling for access between new and old should be kept to a minimum. It is less likely that the overall structure will be caused unnecessary weakening if this tack is taken. Extensions, which do not involve connecting with thatch, are likely to cause fewer problems than those which involve awkward junctions of thatch with some other material or which require valleys. All such connections and junctions are weak points as regards weather-proofing the building.

Traditionally, vernacular houses were extended in length through the addition of a room onto one or both ends of the house. This has resulted in some very long houses (Killeenmore, near Killeigh and Derrinduff, near Crinkill being good examples). Usually the thatched roofs of such houses were simply extended to cover the new room or rooms. Occasionally, the original hipped end of a hipped house is preserved within the extension. For owners intending to extend their houses length-wise today, it would be a good idea to follow such an example. With some houses, the extensions are obvious due to a different roofing material or much thinner (perhaps concrete) walls.

Converting houses to other uses can involve a high degree of adaptation and perhaps much destruction of original fabric. For example, the housing of livestock or farm machinery in disused houses can require the removal of internal walls (including the old kitchen hearth) and the creation of wider openings in outer walls.

Holiday homes have been seen as a desirable reuse of old houses, but nothing can really be better than full-time occupants for keeping the heart in an old house. It is important to note also that the state does not grant aid the re-thatching of houses used as holiday homes.

Protecting Offaly's thatched buildings

The Planning Act 2000 provides the legal basis for the protection of buildings of architectural interest and for the first time obliges all planning authorities to produce a list or record of structures whose protection is regarded as being important to the heritage of the county. The individual buildings are now known as 'Protected Structures' and the list is called the 'Record of Protected Structures (RPS)'. The act also allows for grant aid for owners of Protected Structures. Eight buildings which are, or were, thatched are listed for protection under the Planning Acts in the current *Offaly County Development Plan* (1996) and the *Tullamore Town Development Plan* (1997).

Because of the great vulnerability of thatched buildings in comparison with other historic structures, every effort must be made to retain what is left of this most critical part of the historic building stock of the county. The Heritage Council and others have recommended protection in the development plan lists for all traditional thatched buildings.

In the case of buildings that are currently thatched, inclusion in the Record of Protected Structures should assist the owner with essential repairs to the building. It is also recognition of the cultural importance of thatched buildings for the people of Offaly as a whole. However, the annual amount of direct grant aid for historic buildings from the state is paltry, amounting to only a few million euro, for the entire Republic! On the other hand, the grant aid for thatching under the same department's housing grants schemes has undoubtedly helped hundreds of buildings which would otherwise have been lost.

The Record of Monuments and Places (RMP)[3]

Seventeenth-century and earlier houses are also protected as 'Recorded Monuments' under the National Monuments (Amendment) Act 1994. Most of these buildings are described in the *Archaeological Inventory of Co. Offaly*, published in 1997. Two more houses dating to before AD 1700 became known during the fieldwork for the Offaly Thatch Survey.

Protecting vulnerable thatched buildings
Some of the thatched buildings that are in a poor state of repair are unlikely to be occupied again. Legal protection will not provide these with a roof and will not protect them from neglect or from the elements. It has been suggested that an emergency survey should be carried out to record and survey them before they become too ruinous to record properly.

I would suggest that selected buildings be covered over in corrugated iron to give them protection from the elements until an owner might take on the challenge of repairing and re-thatching them.

Re-thatching of previously-thatched buildings
It should be remembered that thatched roofs are commonly found under corrugated iron and some other materials. The corrugated iron has performed a marvellous job of protecting the thatch and the old roof structures, although the corrugated iron can encourage condensation and rot if a sufficient gap is not left between it and the underlying thatch. Such buildings could be restored as thatched buildings. Hundreds of buildings in Offaly have corrugated iron, asbestos or corrugated felt covering over a thatched roof. Some of the owners of these buildings are keen to see them restored back to the thatch. It should be remembered, especially in the case of roofs that were covered in a long time ago, that there is likely to be an old roof structure present that should be retained. The Department of the Environment, Heritage and Local Government through the thatching grant system, is willing to grant aid the re-thatching of buildings that were previously thatched. Such re-thatching is likely to help the survival of thatching as a craft.

References
1. Oram, Richard, 'Vernacular buildings in Northern Ireland: preservation versus social perception', in Ní Fhloinn, Bairbre and Dennison, Gabriel, *Traditional Architecture in Ireland and its role in rural tourism and development*. Dublin 1994, p. 64.
2. Oram, *op. cit.*, p. 63.
3. The current RMP for Co. Offaly was published in 1995.

8

TIPS FOR HELPING TO KEEP THE THATCH OVER YOUR HEAD[1]

General

Get yourself an experienced and reputable thatcher. Talk to owners of other thatched properties and ask their opinion about work carried out on their buildings.

Do not climb onto or move about thatch unless necessary: This applies also to persons erec-
ting or repairing chimneys, television aerials, etc.

If birds or vermin are making holes in the thatch, ask your thatcher to apply wire netting. If
possible keep this to the ridge and eaves only as otherwise it might inhibit maintenance
of the roof.

The roof pitch should be a minimum of about 50 degrees: Anything less than 45 degrees will
lead to water lodging. Ireland is a wet place and is unlikely to get any drier!

Your thatcher should apply 'Bluestone' (copper sulphate) annually. This helps straw thatch
keep its colour and helps to prevent or kill small insects that might attract birds and other
animals.

*If you own a thatched building but are not in a position to use it or to keep it maintained you might
consider having it covered over (carefully) with corrugated iron. This would ensure that the roof is preserved and could be re-thatched later.*

Materials

Straw for straw and reed for reed

It is important for the survival of straw thatching that buildings which have been traditionally roofed in straw, continue to be so roofed. The same applies to reed in traditional reed
areas. A switch to a different material results in a change of thatching technique and possibly
alterations to the underlying materials and roof structure. A lot of important historical, archaeological and botanical evidence can be lost if the roof is changed. However, it would be per-
verse for the statutory authorities to insist on not using reed, for example, if suitable thatching
straw proves impossible to find. Owners and thatchers traditionally varied the materials, depending on what was available. This is also an essential feature of thatching and building maintenance.

Use real thatch

Industrially produced panels of 'thatch', ready-coated in fire retardant material, are suggested
from time to time. They do not constitute thatch and should be rejected by owners and thatchers. Use of such material would completely undermine the traditional nature of thatching as
a craft. Likewise, thatching over another material, such as slate or corrugated iron or asbestos,
is also very dubious. Such roofs are merely veneers. If the 'thatch' were blown off in a storm,
the roof would still function. In reality, if a person wants a roof of thatch over some other
material, it is their choice, but they will not qualify for a thatching grant.

Use materials grown in a traditional way

Thatchers and owners generally agree that material grown in 'the old fashioned way' is more
suitable and appropriate for thatching. Traditionally, cereal straw was manured naturally. An
age-old balance was achieved which was upset by the emergence of industrial fertilisers and
their over-application has been blamed for all sorts of problems. It would be hard to argue that

they have not increased crop yields, but the emphasis on yield has resulted in a straw weakened by too much nitrogen. A few growers scattered around the country have grown, and will continue to grow, organic thatching material. Where older varieties of straw exist, these should be identified and encouraged, as they are likely to have just the right properties for traditional thatch.

Use materials harvested in the traditional way
The traditional method of harvesting cereals was with the sickle or scythe and later, the reaper-binder. Both of these ensured a long, unbroken straw suitable for thatching. In modern times, the combine-harvester, coupled with the concentration on yield, has produced a shorter, broken and weaker straw of little apparent benefit for thatching. In extreme or emergency circumstances where better straw is not available, it may be acceptable to use bale straw until better materials can be applied.

Maintenance and repair

Apply for grants in good time for effective repair of the roof
It can be a tricky job juggling the grant application with the availability of the thatcher and of thatching materials. The grant is only payable on a seven-year cycle. A good job of thatching should ensure that the roof does not require repair before the period is up. The address and telephone numbers for the housing grants section of the Department of the Environment, Heritage and Local Government are set out in 'Useful Addresses' in the next part of this book.

Learn how to patch your roof!
Talk to your thatcher. He is unlikely to feel that his livelihood is threatened and it is in his interest to ensure that as many roofs as possible last as long as possible. It was also common in former times for owners to be able to do some patching while waiting for a thatcher. This is especially useful when winter storms have caused minor damage to roofs. Of course, extensive damage will require the services of a professional thatcher. Patching is traditional and helped roofs from falling into disrepair.

Avoid allowing trees or hedges to overhang the roof or be unduly close to the roof
The drips can cause advanced decay through continual wetting and drying and build up of leaf and woody debris that can result in water-logging and plant growth.

Avoid letting vegetation grow close to or into thatch
Ivy and creepers may look picturesque climbing onto thatch, but they will cause damage as they burrow their way through. In one case, a creeper had made its way right through to the other side of the roof, displacing and holing the thatch as it went.

Keep cables away from thatch as they can cause damage through flapping and water-logging

Protect the walls with a good overhang
As thatched roofs do not have gutters and down pipes, a good overhang of thatch is essential to protect the walls from run off of rain and snow. This is especially the case for clay ('mud') walls.

Be especially careful with the repair of roof structures
Thatched buildings may have roof structures that are of special significance because of their

historic carpentry. Unwise removal or replacement of parts of such roofs could damage or destroy important historical evidence. It is important to get specialist advice on what parts are essential to the character of the roof.

Fire safety[2]

Roof voids

Ceilings beneath a thatched roof should be sufficiently strong to support fire fighters and their equipment. Access hatches not less than 60cm by 90cm serving the space should be provided. A suitable hatch will also provide the owner with access to enable any fire detection system to be serviced.

A smoke detector should be fitted in the highest point of the roof void (where possible) and this should be linked to a second alarm sited in the hallway or landing. With this type of system, any smoke detected in the roof will sound the alarm in the house.

Hot work should *not* be carried out in the roof void or on the first floor. This includes the use of blow torches and hot air strippers. No naked flames should be allowed in the roof void; the atmosphere in old dusty roof spaces can be highly combustible.

It is most important that electric wiring in the roof space should comply with ETCI rules. Only essential wiring should be run through the roof void. This should be carried in a conduit and not attached to the rafters holding the thatch. Light fittings in the roof space should be enclosed in a bulkhead. Wiring should be checked at least every five years with a keen eye to look for any signs of obvious damage (such as gnawing by rodents) or anything which might present danger of electrical fire.

Any security lighting should be fitted at least 1m (3ft 4in) away from the thatch. Wiring should not be laid through the thatch.

Television aerials preferably should be fitted to a free-standing pole away from the roof. Otherwise, they may be fixed to a gable or gable-end chimney and the cable run down the wall, avoiding any contact with the thatch. Although lightning striking a thatched building is very rare, a lightning conductor may be fitted.

No materials that might increase the potential for fire should be stored in roof spaces.

Chimneys

Great care should be taken in the design and building of chimneys.

All brickwork, mortar and flashing should be regularly checked by a competent builder and any repairs or repointing necessary carried out. This applies particularly to parts of the chimney which are hidden within the thatch, but exposed during re-thatching. Where the chimney is in use, have it swept twice a year for coal-burning fires and quarterly if wood is burnt. Wood used in stoves and on open fires must be well seasoned and dry and it should be stored indoors before use. The top of all chimney pots should be a minimum of 1.8m (6ft) above the ridge. A spark arrestor should be fitted and it is essential that the spark arrestor is kept clean and well maintained as a build up of soot could cause a fire.

Due to the development of more efficient heating systems, draught proofing and insulation, old chimneys are no longer able to cope with the higher temperatures generated. Modern appliances generate high flue gas temperatures which, in the particular case of a single skin brick central chimney in a deep thatch, may ignite the thatch by heat transfer through sound brickwork. Rebuilding should be in double thickness and an appropriate liner must be fitted. Conservation advice should be sought.

Do not have metal boiler flues pass through or close to thatch.

New roofs

New buildings must comply with building regulations and will have fire retardant membranes between thatch and ceiling.

If the roof is completely renewed, the new thatch should be laid over fire resistant insulation board. Any boards or foil should give one hour of fire protection.

General

Do not use or allow the use of naked flames, blow-torches or flame stripping of paint near thatched roofs.

Do not use or allow the use of bonfires, barbecues (usually popular when the thatch is driest) or fireworks near thatched roofs. Such activities should be sited as far as possible from thatched buildings.

Have a hose pipe available to hand and a good source of water. A good pump would also be an advantage to maintain adequate pressure.

When renewing thatch, any old netting should be removed and replaced as necessary, using simple fixings and tyings. This will make it easier for the fire brigade to make a fire break should a fire occur.

It is prudent, when planning extensions or other external works to leave sufficient space around the house to enable the whole roof to be accessible if a fire breaks out.

In the event of a fire

Evacuate the building and call the fire brigade, informing them of the precise address and the nearest main road or landmark and telling them that the building is thatched.

If the fire has started inside the building or in the roof space, do nothing that will increase the draught and on no account remove thatch from the roof. Close all doors and windows as occupants evacuate the building to help prevent the fire from spreading.

If the fire has started outside the building it may be possible, while awaiting the fire brigade, to dampen down the thatch with a garden hose connected to a water supply with sufficient pressure and without endangering personal safety.

Other issues

When repairing or altering a historic building, there are a few basic principles which apply:

Retain original features

A vernacular building which has been 'gutted' internally, perhaps involving the removal of the hearth wall, is of very little real cultural heritage value. The internal layout of the traditional house, for example, is important and distinguishes it fundamentally from all other house types. It is also important to retain traditional timber battened (boarded) or panelled doors, timber sash windows, traditional hearths and other internal fittings/furniture and decorative features. Much of this was the work of journeymen joiners. The items of furniture, such as the dresser, settle bed, wall racks, box beds, etc., are of cultural value. Such items are of less heritage value when taken out of their natural milieu – the traditional house for which they were often specially made.

Replace like with like

Timber sash windows rarely have to be entirely replaced. When they need repair, it is usually possible for a good carpenter to replace the broken or rotten piece. In this way, such windows are immeasurably less wasteful than modern aluminium and uPVC types, which when broken usually need to be entirely discarded and replaced. Timber windows are far less toxic to manufacture and dispose of and of course can be recycled. Likewise, lime-wash and lime-plaster should be replaced with the same materials. Lime allows an old wall to 'breathe' whereas concrete does not. Water penetration through cracks in concrete will eventually lead to the whole render failing.

If it's not broken, don't fix it!
Leave well enough alone! Don't be tempted to throw good money after bad when renovating an old building. Talk to the conservation officer – he or she will probably save you a lot of money!

Good drainage
This is very important. Buildings constructed into a hillside or sloping ground are notoriously prone to dampness and ingress of water. A well-constructed drain between slope and building walls should enable the building to dry out and stay dry. Seek advice from the conservation officer and/or a reputable builder with experience of old buildings.

Don't use chemical or other sealants on walls or roofs
These materials, which are peddled as a panacea for all sorts of ailments, are to be avoided. Anything that works against the natural ability of a building to breathe, that is to absorb and shed moisture gradually, may prevent the building from so doing. In the long term such sealant are likely to cause serious harm to the building and expense for the owner.

Keep your render
It may be tempting to strip the render off a building to expose the stonework. Again, Ireland has a wet climate! The render is there for a very good reason. Stripping render and exposing stone, which was never meant to be exposed, will lead to deterioration of the stonework in a relatively short time. This is exacerbated if the stonework is then re-pointed in hard cement mortars.

Seek advice from your local authority conservation officer or planning department – this cannot be emphasised enough. If the local authority does not have in-house staff expert in the area of traditional buildings they should be able to refer queries onto someone who does have such expertise.

References
1. Society for the Protection of Ancient Buildings and the Rural Development Commission. *Technical Pamphlet 10. The Care and Repair of Thatched Roofs*. London 1986. Authors Peter Brockett and Adela Wright; Environment Service; www.thatch.org
2. I am also most grateful to the Offaly County Fire Service for their advice.

9

GAZETTEER OF THATCHED BUILDINGS IN OFFALY

1 **'Hennessy's', Main Street, Ferbane**   **Public house**   **Altered**
Terraced multiple-bay single-storey public house, formerly a dwelling, with later shop-front built pre-1838. Fronts onto street. Lobby-entry plan. Roughcast rendered stone walls and pitched reed roof with modern detailing to front and slate roof to rear. Rendered brick chimneys. Timber sash windows and panelled door with fan-light and side-lights. Timber shop-front with panelled and glazed double door, panelled pilasters and fascia.

2 **The Mallet Tavern, Kilbride Street, Tullamore**   **Public house**   **Altered**
Terraced four-bay two-storey thatched public house built pre-1838. Fronts onto street. Plan form altered and walls raised. Rendered walls with pitched modern reed roof with raised ridge and exposed scolloping. Rendered concrete chimneys. Replacement timber windows and double door. The only two-storey thatched building in Co. Offaly and the only thatched roof in Tullamore.

3 **Lynally Glebe townland, near Mucklagh**   **House**
Detached four-bay single-storey thatched house built pre-1838. Set at right angles to road. Direct-entry plan. Lime-washed rendered stone walls. Pitched oaten straw roof with exposed scolloping to ridge. Rendered concrete chimneys. Replacement timber windows to front, timber sash to rear. Timber panelled door.

4 **Clonavoe townland, near Clonbullogue**   **House**
Detached five-bay single-storey thatched farmhouse built pre-1838. Set at right angles to road. Direct-entry plan. Pebble-dashed rendered clay walls. Hipped oaten straw roof with knotted ridge and exposed scolloping to ridge and eaves and wire to eaves. Rendered concrete chimneys. Timber sash windows. Windbreak with flat concrete canopy with replacement timber and glazed door is an addition. Northernmost bay is an addition and has a hipped, corrugated iron roof. Modern extension to rear with flat felt roof.

5 **Clonavoe townland, near Clonbullogue**   **House**
Detached four-bay single-storey thatched house built pre-1838. Set at right angles to road. Direct-entry plan. Pebble-dashed clay walls. Hipped oaten straw roof with knotted ridge with end bobbins and exposed scolloping to ridge and eaves. Rendered concrete chimney. Timber sash windows. Replacement timber and glazed door. Extension to rear with flat felt roof.

6 **Clonroosk Big townland, near Clonbullogue**   **House**
Detached four-bay single-storey thatched farmhouse built pre-1838. Faces road and its farmyard. Direct-entry plan. Roughcast rendered walls. Hipped oaten straw roof with bobbins and exposed scolloping to ridge and eaves. Rendered concrete chimney. Replacement timber windows. Replacement timber and glazed door in windbreak with flat concrete roof.

7 **Moneenagunnell townland, near Belmont**   **House**   **Ruinous**
Detached four-bay single-storey thatched farmhouse built pre-1838. Faces road with garden in between. Direct-entry plan. Lime-washed and lime-plastered stone walls. Pitched scolloped oaten straw roof, collapsing in. Rendered brick chimneys. Timber sash windows. Timber battened door and half-door.

8 **Killeenmore townland, near Killeigh**   **House**
Detached six-bay single-storey thatched farmhouse built pre-1838. Set at right angles to road and faces its farmyard. Lobby-entry plan. Pebble-dashed stone walls. Pitched oaten

straw roof. Rendered concrete and brick chimneys. Timber casement windows. Timber battened door in two-bay porch and extension with lean-to corrugated asbestos roof. Southernmost bay converted to a shed in 1954; door inserted into the gable and internal door blocked up. The longest thatched house in Co. Offaly.

9   **Clonmore townland, near Bracknagh**   House
Detached four-bay, single-storey thatched farmhouse built pre-1838. Faces road with garden in between. Altered plan. Pebble-dashed clay walls. Pitched (N) and hipped (S) oaten straw roof with knotted ridge with end finials and plastic conduit to ridge and eaves. Rendered concrete over brick chimneys. Timber sash windows. Porch with flat concrete roof is an addition and has a timber panelled and glazed door, replacing earlier doorway, which was located between the southernmost windows. Extensions to rear in late 1950s (S), 1968 (N). Extension to N gable has concrete walls and a pitched slate roof. Northernmost bay of thatched part also has concrete walls. Original house appears to have been of four bays and doubled in size since.

10 **Ballydownan townland, Geashill**   House
Detached five-bay two-pile single-storey thatched house built between 1838–1912. Set at right angles to road. Lobby-entry plan. Pebble-dashed walls. Pitched oaten straw roof with exposed scolloping to ridges and wire to eaves. Timber casement windows; canted bay with thatched canopy to gable. Windbreak with timber battened door with pitched oaten straw roof. Rendered chimney. Second pile may be an addition and has similar roof and window detailing. Conservatory extension to rear.

11 **The Ould Thatch, Hill Street, Cloghan**   Public house   Gone
End of terrace seven-bay two-storey thatched public house, built pre-1838, demolished 2002. Fronted onto street. Altered plan form. Rendered stone walls, roughcast to first floor. Pitched oaten straw roof. Rendered brick chimneys. Replacement uPVC windows and timber doors. Timber shop-front of c. 1900 altered c. 1960s. Formerly Kilcommons public house at W end and grocery/ newsagent at E end.

12 **Killurin townland, Killurin**   House
Detached four-bay single-storey farmhouse with loft over N end built pre-1838. Backs onto road and faces into its farmyard. Lobby-entry plan. Rendered stone walls. Pitched oaten straw roof. Exposed brick chimneys. Replacement aluminium windows. Windbreak with flat concrete canopy and timber battened door. Northernmost bay converted to workshop.

13 **Hawkswood townland, near Killeigh**   House
Detached four-bay single-storey thatched former farmhouse. Built pre-1838. Set at right angles to road and faces former farmyard. Direct-entry plan. Pebble-dashed stone walls. Pitched oaten straw roof with exposed scolloping to ridge and twine to eaves. Rendered chimneys. Timber sash windows. Porch with flat concrete roof, sash windows and timber battened door. One-bay extension to rear with pitched tiled roof with flat-roofed link to original building.

14 **Ballykean townland, near Geashill**   House   Ruinous
Detached four-bay single-storey ruinous thatched farmhouse with loft over W end. At end of avenue and in middle of farmyard. Built pre-1838. Lobby-entry plan. Roughcast rendered clay over stone walls. Pitched scolloped oaten straw thatched roof but without scraw under-thatch. Rendered brick chimneys. Timber sash windows. Remains of concrete porch. Western part of building has collapsed. One-bay recessed extension to W end with pitched slate roof.

15 **Killeigh townland, near Killeigh**   House
Detached four-bay single-storey thatched house. Built pre-1838. Lobby-entry plan. Hipped oaten straw thatched roof with bobbins and exposed scolloping to ridge. Rendered

walls. Replacement uPVC windows. Timber door. Rendered chimney. One-bay extension with pitched tiled roof and more recent extension with flat tiled roof to rear.

16 Urney townland, near Clonygowan   **House**

Detached four-bay single-storey thatched house. Faces road with forecourt in between. Built pre-1838. Lobby-entry plan. Pebble-dashed stone walls. Pitched (S end) and hipped (N end) oaten straw roof with plastic conduit to ridge and twine to eaves. Rendered chimneys. Replacement timber windows and timber panelled door. Building may have been extended southwards as that part is recessed slightly.

17 Sranure, near Clonygowan   **House**

Detached three-bay single-storey thatched farmhouse. Faces road with garden in between. Built pre-1838. Lobby-entry plan. Roughcast rendered walls. Pitched oaten straw roof with bobbins and exposed scolloping to ridge and W end and twine to eaves. Rendered chimney. Timber sash windows. No windows to rear wall. Porch with flat concrete roof with timber panelled door. Extension to rear with flat concrete roof.

18 Dan and Molly's, Ballyboy   **Public house**

Detached six-bay single-storey thatched public house at corner location in village. Built pre-1838. Fronts onto street. Rendered stone walls. Pitched oaten straw roof with wide overhang and decorative bobbins and exposed scolloping to ridge and twine to eaves. Rendered chimney. Timber sash windows. Timber panelled doors. Painted sign at eaves.

19 Knocknahorna, near Birr   **House**   **Ruinous**

Detached four-bay single-storey ruinous thatched farmhouse. Built pre-1838. Faces road with yard in between and outbuildings to side. Direct-entry plan. Pitched oaten straw roof. Brick chimneys. Stone walls. Timber sash windows. Porch with concrete walls and flat concrete roof with timber and glazed door. Northern half of roof has collapsed.

20 Ballaghanoher townland, near Birr   **House**

Detached two-bay single-storey T-plan thatched farmhouse. Backs to road with large garden in between and faces into farmyard. Built pre-1838. Direct-entry plan. Rendered stone walls. Pitched oaten straw roof. One-bay return at rear with pitched oaten straw roof. Rendered chimney. Replacement timber and sash windows. Porch with flat concrete roof and replacement timber windows and replacement timber panelled and glazed door with side-lights. Part of roof collapsed 2002. Known as 'Horan's of the Hollow'.

21 Rathure South townland, near Killyon, Birr   **House**

Detached four-bay single-storey thatched farmhouse. Faces road with yard in between and farm buildings to side and rear. Built pre-1838. Lobby-entry plan. Lime-washed (front) and exposed (rear) stone walls. Pitched oaten straw roof. Rendered chimneys. Timber sash windows. Timber vertically divided battened door.

22 'The Thatch', Crinkill   **Public house**

Detached seven-bay single-storey thatched public house, formerly dwelling house. Faces onto street. Built pre-1838. Lobby-entry plan. Rendered stone walls. Pitched reed roof with raised ridge with exposed scolloping. Timber sash windows. Two brick porches with pitched thatched roofs and timber panelled doors. Rendered chimneys. Rear extension has concrete walls and pitched thatched roof. Southern porch is post-1910.

23 Derrinduff townland, near Crinkill   **House**

Detached six-bay single-storey thatched former farmhouse. Set at right angles to road and facing into former farmyard, now a garden. Built pre-1838. Roughcast stone walls. Pitched reed roof with raised ridge with decorative scolloping. Rendered chimney. Timber sash windows. Windbreak with flat concrete canopy and replacement timber panelled door. Interior altered. Northern two bays formerly a farm building. One-bay extension to rear with pitched tiled roof and rendered chimney; smaller extension with lean-to corrugated steel roof.

24 Ballyegan townland, near Sharavogue, Birr   House

Detached five-bay single-storey thatched farmhouse. Faces onto road with farm buildings to side and rear. Built pre-1838. Lobby-entry plan. Lime-washed lime-plastered walls with heavy stone buttress to NE corner. Pitched oaten straw roof with exposed scolloping to ridge. Rendered chimneys. Timber sash windows. Windbreak sheltered under thatch with timber panelled door. Extension to rear with concrete walls and pitched slated roof. Shed with stone walls and pitched corrugated iron roof added to N gable.

25 Garrymona townland, near Walsh Island   House

Detached four-bay single-storey thatched former farmhouse. Set at right angles to road. Built pre-1838. Direct-entry plan. Rendered stone walls. Half-hipped reed roof with raised ridge with exposed scolloping. One rendered chimney. Replacement timber windows. Exposed cut stone windbreak with pitched slate roof and replacement timber battened door and half-door. Extension (to form L-plan building) built 1999 has concrete walls and pitched thatched roof. Smaller thatched house in yard was formerly an outbuilding (see No. 26).

26 Garrymona townland, near Walsh Island   House

Detached two-bay single-storey thatched house, formerly outbuilding. In yard with No. 25. Built pre-1838. Rendered stone walls. Half-hipped reed roof with raised ridge with exposed scolloping. Replacement timber windows. Exposed cut stone windbreak with pitched slate roof and replacement timber battened halved door.

27 Ballinvoher townland, near Clonygowan   House

Detached four-bay single-storey thatched farmhouse. Built pre-1838. Direct-entry plan. Set at right angles to road with farm buildings opposite and to side. Roughcast stone walls. Pitched oaten straw roof with bobbins and plastic conduit to ridge and twine to eaves. Rendered chimneys. Timber sash windows. Porch with flat corrugated iron roof and timber battened door. A further bay at W end collapsed 1998.

28 Ballydownan townland, near Geashill   House

Detached four-bay single-storey thatched former farmhouse. Built pre-1838. At end of an avenue. Direct-entry plan. Lime-washed lime-plastered clay walls. Heavy stone buttress to rear wall. Hipped oaten straw roof with twine to eaves. Rendered chimney. Timber pivoted windows. Timber battened door. Slightly recessed southern bay appears to be an extension. Small shed with lean-to corrugated iron roof to N end of house.

29 Bogtown townland, near Clonygowan   House

Detached four-bay single-storey thatched former miller's house, lofted over S end. Built pre-1838. Faces road with garden/yard in between. Direct-entry plan. Rendered stone walls. Pitched reed roof with raised ridge with exposed scolloping. Rendered concrete chimney. Replacement timber windows. Porch with hipped (formerly cat-slide) thatched roof, fixed windows in side walls and replacement timber halved battened door with side-lights. Former outbuilding with stone walls and pitched roof incorporated into house to form L-plan building connected to original with glass and timber link. Northern bay appears to be an addition as roof pitch is lower.

30 Murragh townland, near Rahan   House

Detached four-bay single-storey thatched farmhouse. Built pre-1838. Faces into farmyard at end of avenue. Lobby-entry plan. Pebble-dashed stone walls. Pitched oaten straw roof with bobbins and exposed scolloping to ridge and twine to eaves. Rendered chimneys. Timber sash windows. Porch with pitched slate roof, windows in side walls and timber panelled door with side-lights. Farm building with concrete walls and pitched corrugated iron roof attached to N gable.

31 Galros townland, near Cloghan   House

Detached four-bay single-storey thatched former farmhouse. Built pre-1838. Faces road with yard in between. Pebble-dashed stone walls. Pitched oaten straw roof with bobbins and exposed scolloping to ridge and twine to eaves. Rendered chimneys. Replacement uPVC windows. Timber battened door and half door. One-bay extension to rear with concrete walls and pitched tiled roof.

32 Annaghmore townland, near Highstreet, Belmont   House
Detached five-bay single-storey thatched farmhouse. Built pre-1838. Faces road with garden in between. Formerly backed onto road and faced into farmyard. Direct-entry, formerly lobby-entry plan. Roughcast rendered walls. Pitched oaten straw roof with exposed scolloping to ridge and eaves. Rendered chimneys. Replacement uPVC windows and doors. South-western bay is an extension and has concrete walls and pitched slated roof.

33 Killurin townland, near Killurin   House
Detached three-bay single-storey thatched house. Built pre-1838. Fronts onto roadside. Lobby-entry plan. Lime-washed and lime-plastered stone walls. Hipped oaten straw roof with bobbins and exposed scolloping to ridge and twine to eaves. Rendered chimney. Pivoted steel windows; no windows in rear (N) wall. Timber battened door and half-door.

34 Killellery townland, near Geashill   House
Detached six-bay single-storey thatched farmhouse. Built pre-1838. Faces road with garden in between and farm buildings to side and rear. Lobby-entry plan. Lime-washed lime-plastered clay walls. Hipped oaten straw roof. Rendered chimneys. Pivoted steel windows (front) and timber sash (rear). Windbreak with lean-to corrugated iron canopy with replacement timber battened door.

35 Garbally townland, near Mount Bolus   House
Detached multiple-bay two-storey thatched house of irregular plan built c. 2000. Faces road with large garden in between. Exposed random limestone-faced walls. Pitched and conical reed roofs with raised ridges with decorative scolloping. Brick chimney. Timber windows and timber battened doors.

36 Cappancur townland, near Tullamore   House
Detached four-bay single-storey thatched farmhouse. Built pre-1838. Faces road with garden in between and farm buildings to side and rear. Lobby-entry plan. Rendered stone walls. Pitched oaten straw roof with bobbins and exposed scolloping to ridge and twine to eaves. Rendered chimney. Former farm building with stone walls and pitched slate roof incorporated into house to form L-plan. Large flat corrugated roof extension to full length of rear of house. Timber sash windows. Windbreak with gabled thatched canopy with timber panelled and glazed door.

37 Knockballyboy townland, near Daingean   House
Detached five-bay single-storey thatched house. Built pre-1838 (and probably post-Grand Canal). Faces and is parallel to Grand Canal towpath with garden in between. Lobby-entry plan. Roughcast rendered walls. Pitched oaten straw roof with bobbins and exposed scolloping to ridge and exposed scolloping to eaves. Rendered chimneys. Replacement timber windows (front) and timber sash windows (rear). Porch with concrete walls and flat concrete roof with timber panelled door.

38 Main Street, Shannonbridge   House   Altered
Detached four-bay single-storey with loft thatched house. Built pre-1838, remodelled and roof raised 2000. Faces onto street at corner location. Exposed random limestone-faced walls. Pitched reed roof with raised ridge with exposed scolloping. Brick chimney. Replacement timber windows. Replacement timber battened halved door.

39 Coolcor townland, near Rhode   House
Detached five-bay single-storey thatched house. Built pre-1838. Faces road with fore-

court in between. Direct-entry plan. Roughcast rendered walls. Hipped oaten straw roof with bobbins, end finials and plastic conduit to ridge and hips and plastic conduit to eaves. Rendered chimney. Replacement uPVC windows and door. Extension at rear with flat felt roof.

40 **Ballygaddy townland, near Sharavogue, Birr**   House   **Ruinous**
Detached five-bay single-story ruinous thatched farmhouse. Built pre-1838. Set at right angles to road with farm buildings opposite and yard in between. Lobby-entry plan. Random uncoursed stone walls with remains of lime-plaster; rear wall much collapsed. Remains of pitched oaten straw roof. Remains of timber sash windows. Porch with brick walls and pitched corrugated iron roof; door gone. Two eastern bays appear to have been farm buildings originally, later incorporated into house.

41 **Clonmeen townland, near Rhode**   House
Detached four-bay single-storey thatched house. Built pre-1838. Faces road with garden in between. Altered plan. Pebble-dashed stone walls. Hipped (N end) and pitched (S end) oaten straw roof with bobbins and exposed scolloping to ridge. S end has tiles under the thatch. Brick chimneys. Replacement timber windows. Extension to rear with flat felt roof. Timber panelled door. Southern two bays appear to be an extension.

42 **Coolnagrower townland, near Birr**   House
Conjoined four-bay single-storey thatched farmhouse. Built pre-1838. Set at an angle to road with garden in between. Farmyard to side. Direct-entry plan. Pebble-dashed stone walls. Pitched oaten straw roof with exposed scolloping to ridge. Rendered chimneys. Replacement timber windows (front) and timber sash (rear). Timber panelled door. Farm building with pebble-dashed walls and pitched corrugated asbestos roof attached to NE end of house.

43 **Cloncoher townland, near Geashill**   House
Detached four-bay single-storey thatched farmhouse with integral one-bay farm building. Built pre-1838. Faces road with garden in between. Outbuildings to rear. Direct-entry plan. Lime-washed lime-plastered walls with concrete plinth at W gable. Pitched (E end) and hipped (W end) oaten straw roof with exposed scolloping to ridge. Rendered chimney. Steel pivoted windows. Porch with concrete walls (replacing earlier windbreak with timber battened door) and flat corrugated iron roof with timber panelled door. 'Portacabin' at rear provides further accommodation and is linked to original house by flat-roofed connection.

44 **Derrybeg townland, near Killeigh**   House
Detached five-bay single-storey thatched farmhouse. Built pre-1838. Faces road with yard between. Direct-entry plan. Rendered clay walls. Hipped oaten straw roof with bobbins and exposed scolloping to ridge. Rendered chimney. One-bay entrance bay with concrete walls and hipped thatched roof. Steel pivoted windows. Replacement uPVC door.

45 **Clonsast Lower townland, near Bracknagh**   House
Detached six-bay single-storey thatched former farmhouse. Built pre-1838. Faces road with garden in between. Altered lobby-entry plan. Rendered clay walls. Pitched oaten straw roof with exposed scolloping to ridge and eaves. Rendered chimneys. Replacement uPVC windows. Porch with pitched thatched roof. Two former outbuildings to rear of house with rendered walls and pitched artificial slate roofs incorporated into house; small extension also added. House known as 'The Spinning Wheel'.

46 **Cloncon townland, near Tullamore**   House
Conjoined four-bay single-storey thatched farmhouse. Built pre-1838. Set at right angles to road and faces into parallel farmyard. Direct-entry plan. Lime-washed lime-plastered clay walls. Pitched (N end) and hipped (S end) oaten straw roof with decorative bobbins to ridge and exposed scolloping to ridge and eaves. Rendered brick chimneys. Timber

sash windows. Timber battened door and sheet half-door. One-bay outbuilding with stone walls and pitched corrugated iron roof added to N end of house.

47 Killaun townland, near Birr   House   Ruinous

Detached four-bay partly thatched ruinous farmhouse. Built pre-1838. Faces into yard at end of avenue. Direct-entry plan. Roughcast rendered random stone walls. Pitched ruinous oaten straw (southern bay) and tile (other bays) roof. Rendered chimneys. Replacement timber windows. Timber panelled door. One-bay outbuilding with concrete walls and lean-to roof attached to S end of house.

48 Kilcummin townland, near Highstreet, Belmont   House   Ruinous

Detached four-bay single-storey with loft (over W end) ruinous thatched house. Built pre-1838. Faces road with forecourt in between. Outbuilding to side/front. Direct-entry plan. Rendered stone walls. Pitched ruinous oaten straw roof. Rendered brick chimneys. Timber sash windows. Remains of timber battened door. For sale 2002.

49 Derrinclare townland, near Shinrone   House

Detached four-bay single-storey thatched house. Built pre-1838. Set at right angles to road. Large garden to rear and yard to front of house. Direct-entry plan. Rendered walls. Pitched reed roof with exposed scolloping to ridge. Rendered chimney. Recent extension with hipped (E end) and half-hipped (W end) reed roof with timber sash windows and timber door added to N end to form L-plan. Timber sash windows. Shallow windbreak with timber post sides and canopy with timber battened door. For sale in 2002.

50 Noggusduff townland, Gallen, Ferbane   House   Ruinous

Conjoined four-bay pitched partly thatched farmhouse. Built pre-1838 (and probably post-Grand Canal). Set at an angle to road with garden and Grand Canal towpath between. Direct-entry plan. Roughcast rendered stone walls. Pitched oaten straw (western three bays) and patterned tile (eastern bay) roof. Rendered brick chimneys; one collapsed. Timber sash windows. Timber battened door.

51 Broughal townland, near Kilcormac   House

Detached five-bay single-storey partly thatched farmhouse. Built pre-1838. Faces yard at end of avenue off lane. Direct-entry plan. Roughcast rendered stone walls. Pitched oaten straw (southern three bays) and tiled (northern two bays) roof. Rendered chimneys. Timber sash windows. Timber battened door and half-door. Part of a pair of farmyards – see No. 52.

52 Broughal townland, near Kilcormac   House

Detached four-bay single-storey thatched farmhouse with one-bay integral outbuilding. Built pre-1838. Faces yard at end of avenue off lane. Direct-entry plan. Roughcast rendered (front) and lime-washed (rear) stone walls with two stone buttresses to rear. Pitched oaten straw roof. Rendered chimneys. Timber sash windows. Timber battened door and half-door. Part of a pair of farmyards – see No. 51.

53 Stonestown townland, near Cloghan   House   Ruinous

Detached four-bay single-storey ruinous thatched farmhouse. Built pre-1838. Faces road with yard of outbuildings in between. Direct-entry plan. Lime-washed lime-plastered walls with stone buttresses to rear. Pitched oaten straw roof, partly collapsed and rear of roof covered in corrugated steel. Rendered chimneys. Timber sash windows. Timber battened door and half-door.

54 Kinagall townland, near Kilcormac   House   Ruinous

Detached four-bay single-storey (with lofts) ruinous thatched farmhouse. Built pre-1838. Lobby-entry plan. Faces into garden with yard of outbuildings to rear at end of avenue. Rendered stone walls; W gable is Pullagh brick. Pitched oaten straw roof. Brick and concrete chimneys. Remains of timber sash windows. Windbreak with gabled canopy with timber battened door. Later porch with concrete walls and lean-to corrugated iron roof.

55 Castletown and Glinsk townland, near Kinnitty   House

Detached farm building rebuilt as house 2002. Original building pre-1838. In grounds of Kinnitty Castle at end of avenue. Four-bay single-storey with loft house. Exposed coursed random stone walls. Pitched reed roof with decorative scolloping to ridge. Exposed stone chimney to rear roof slope. Timber lattice windows; eyebrow windows to eaves. Timber battened door.

56 Killeigh townland, near Killeigh   House

Conjoined four-bay single-storey thatched farmhouse. Built pre-1838. Faces into yard of outbuildings at end of avenue. Lobby-entry plan. Roughcast rendered clay walls. Pitched oaten straw roof with bobbins to ridge and exposed scolloping to ridge and eaves. Rendered chimneys. Timber sash windows. Porch with flat concrete canopy with timber battened door.

57 Derrybeg townland, near Killeigh   House

Detached four-bay single-storey thatched house. Built pre-1838 and extended into courtyard, c. 2000. Faces road with garden in between. Altered direct-entry plan. Rendered walls. Hipped (S end) and pitched (N end) reed roof with decorative scolloping to ridge. Rendered chimney. Replacement timber windows. Windbreak with flat concrete canopy with replacement timber battened door. Extensions to rear with thatched roofs form U-plan, closed by smaller sheds with pitched slate roofs and wrought iron gateway.

58 Derrybeg townland, near Killeigh   House

Detached four-bay single-storey thatched former farmhouse. Built pre-1838. Set at right angles to road with yard to front and outbuildings to side. Direct-entry plan. Roughcast rendered walls. Pitched oaten straw roof with bobbins and exposed scolloping to ridge. Rendered chimneys. Steel pivoted windows. Timber battened door and half-door.

59 Ballydrohid townland, near Tullamore   House   Ruinous

Detached five-bay single-storey with loft ruinous thatched farmhouse. Built pre-1838. Faces garden with extensive farm complex to side and rear at end of avenue off Grand Canal towpath. Lobby-entry plan. Rendered stone walls. Pitched oaten straw roof. Rendered chimneys. Timber sash windows. Timber panelled door. Two-bay extension to rear with rendered walls and lean-to slated roof.

60 Loughroe townland, near Rahan   House

Detached five-bay single-storey thatched (over slate) house. Built pre-1838. Set at right angles to road and faces into garden. Pitched reed over asbestos-cement slate roof with raised ridge with decorative scolloping. Exposed brick chimneys. Timber sash windows. Recessed entrance with replacement timber halved batten door. Extension at rear with flat felt roof.

61 Kilgortin townland, near Rahan   House

Detached six-bay single-storey thatched farmhouse. Built pre-1838 (and probably post-Grand Canal). Faces and is parallel to Grand Canal towpath with garden in between. Direct-entry plan, but may formerly have been lobby-entry and facing into yard. Rendered stone walls. Pitched oaten straw roof with bobbins and exposed scolloping to ridge and twine to eaves. Rendered chimneys. Timber sash windows. Timber panelled door. Extension to rear with flat corrugated iron roof. Stone wheel guard at SE corner.

62 Ballybruncullin townland, near Ballycumber   House

Detached four-bay single-storey thatched farmhouse. Built pre-1838. Faces into yard at end of avenue. Direct-entry plan but with screen wall to one side of entrance internally. Rendered stone walls. Pitched oaten straw roof with exposed scolloping to ridge and twine to eaves. Rendered chimneys. Replacement uPVC windows. Timber door.

63 Aghananagh townland, near Rahan   House

Detached four-bay single-storey thatched farmhouse. Built pre-1838. Faces road with yard in between and outbuildings to side. Direct-entry plan. Rendered stone walls. Pitched rye straw roof with decorative scolloping to slightly raised ridge and chimney. Rendered chimney. Formerly a loft over E end. Timber sash windows. Porch with pitched slate roof with timber door. Extension to rear with rendered walls and pitched slate roof. Shed added to E gable with stone walls and lean-to roof.

64 Cappancur townland, near Tullamore House

Detached four-bay single-storey thatched former farmhouse. Built pre-1838. Faces into yard at end of avenue with outbuildings to front and side. Direct-entry plan. Rendered stone walls; large buttresses to N gable. Pitched oaten straw roof with bobbins and exposed scolloping to ridge and twine to eaves. Rendered chimney. Timber sash and replacement metal windows. Porch with concrete walls and flat concrete roof with timber battened door. Small shed attached to S gable.

65 Turraun townland, near Pollagh House Gone

Detached three-bay single-storey house demolished 2002. Built between 1838–1912. Faced road with small garden in between. Direct-entry plan. Rendered Pullagh brick walls. Pitched oaten straw roof. Rendered brick chimney. Timber sash windows. Timber battened door. Smallest thatched house recorded during the survey.

66 Lea More townland, near Pollagh House

Detached three-bay single-storey house. Built between 1838–1912. At end of avenue. Direct-entry plan. Rendered Pullagh brick walls; rear wall falling out. Pitched oaten straw roof. Rendered chimney. Replacement timber sash windows. Timber battened and glazed door. One-bay extension added to S end with concrete walls and flat felt roof in 1985. Former bay at N end collapsed. Portacabin replacement accommodation next to house.

67 Bawnmore townland, near Geashill House

Detached four-bay single-storey thatched farmhouse. Built pre-1838. Faces into yard at end of avenue. Lobby-entry plan. Pebble-dashed walls. Pitched (NW end) and hipped (SE end) oaten straw roof with bobbins and exposed scolloping to ridge and twine to eaves. Rendered concrete chimney. Replacement timber windows. Windbreak with thatch of roof projecting over with timber panelled door.

68 Ballycue townland, near Geashill House

Detached three-bay single-storey thatched farmhouse. Built pre-1838. Faces garden with outbuildings to rear and side at end of avenue. Altered direct-entry plan. Roughcast rendered walls. Pitched oaten straw roof with bobbins and exposed scolloping to ridge and exposed scolloping to eaves. Rendered chimneys. Replacement uPVC windows (2000). Porch with flat felt roof with replacement uPVC door. One-bay extension to W end and larger to rear wall of house with rendered concrete walls and lean-to corrugated iron and flat felt roofs. Present entrance with timber panelled door in extension. Two-bay extension to E end with rendered concrete walls and pitched slate roof.

69 Ballyduff South townland, near Ballinagar Farm building

Detached two-bay single-storey thatched farm building, used as hen house and shed. Built 1949–50. In farmyard at end of avenue. Timber sleepers and round and split timber posts with painted timber plank and corrugated iron cladding. Hipped oaten straw roof with exposed scolloping to ridge. Timber battened doors in S gable and timber battened half-door in front wall.

70 Ballyduff South townland, near Ballinagar Farm building

Detached three-bay single-storey thatched farmhouse, now in use as farm storage building. Built 1838–1912. At edge of farmyard at end of avenue. Lime-washed and lime-plastered clay and stone walls. Hipped oaten straw roof with exposed scolloping to ridge and eaves. No chimney survives. Timber battened door and double doors in front wall and door-less double ope in W gable. Windows blocked up.

71 **Ballyduff South townland, near Ballinagar**   **Farm building**
Detached one-bay single-storey thatched farm building, used as hay barn and shed. Built 1838–1912. In farmyard at end of avenue. Lime-washed and lime-plastered clay walls. Hipped oaten straw roof with exposed scolloping to ridge. Timber battened door in front wall. Pivoted window to rear. Shed with concrete walls and lean-to corrugated iron roof attached to E end.

72 **Ballyduff South townland, near Ballinagar**   **Farm building**
Detached four-bay single-storey thatched farm building, used as hay barn, hen house and calf shed. Built pre-1838 (W part); extended pre-1912. In farmyard at end of avenue. Lime-washed and lime-plastered clay walls. Hipped oaten straw roof with bobbins and exposed scolloping to ridge. Timber battened door and two door-less opes in front wall. Small unglazed window in rear wall.

73 **Derryweelan townland, near Geashill**   **House**
Detached five-bay single-storey lofted (S end) thatched farmhouse. Built pre-1838. Lobby-entry plan. In farmyard at end of avenue. Rendered clay walls. Pitched oaten straw roof with exposed scolloping to ridge. Rendered chimney. Porch with flat felt roof with timber and glazed door. Replacement uPVC windows. Two large extensions with concrete walls and flat felt and corrugated iron roofs to rear.

74 **Enaghan townland, near Walsh Island**   **House**
Detached three-bay single-storey thatched house. Built pre-1838. Direct-entry plan. Set at right angles to road. Rendered stone walls. Pitched oaten straw roof. Rendered chimney. Timber sash windows. Replacement timber battened halved door. One-bay extension added to E end has rendered walls and pitched tile roof.

75 **Lea Beg townland, near Kilcormac**   **Bird hide**
Detached octagonal-plan thatched bird watcher's hide. Built c. 1999 by Bord na Móna. Faces road and is approached by timber bridge supported on timber posts. Timber plank walls supported on round timber posts. Conical reed roof with raised ridge with decorative scolloping. Narrow horizontal viewing windows in sides. Timber plank double door in front side.

76 **Bracklin Little, near Tullamore**   **House**
Detached four-bay single-storey thatched farmhouse. Built pre-1838. Direct-entry plan. At end of long avenue. Rendered stone walls. Pitched scolloped reed roof over oaten straw. Rendered chimneys. Replacement uPVC windows and replacement battened door. Two-bay flat-roofed extension added to rear 1940s and 1960s.

77 **Killaghintober, near Ballycumber**   **House**
Detached four-bay single-storey thatched farmhouse. Built pre-1838. At end of short avenue close to disused Kilbeggan branch of the Grand Canal. Lobby-entry plan. Eastern bay is later addition and has tiled roof and replacement uPVC windows. Rendered stone walls. Pitched oaten straw roof. Rendered chimneys. Timber sash windows and timber and glazed door.

78 **Ross, near Tullamore**   **Domestic garage**
Detached two-bay thatched garage/storage shed. Built 2002. Steel stanchion and timber sleeper and cladding construction. Half-hipped reed roof with raised ridge.

79 **Cloniff, near Clonmacnoise**   **Bird hide**
Detached two-bay single-storey thatched bird hide. Built c. 2000. Single space internally. In bogland and part of Bord na Móna bog trail. Pitched reed roof. Timber post and clad walls. Timber battened door and fixed windows.

80 **Ballinagar** **House**

Detached five-bay single-storey thatched farmhouse. Built pre-1838. In farmyard. Lobby-entry plan. Jamb wall has two spy windows. Hipped oaten straw roof. Rendered chimney and rendered clay walls. Timber sash windows. Timber panelled door in concrete porch with flat concrete roof. Extension to rear with flat corrugated iron roof.

81 **Castletown** **House**

Detached five-bay single-storey thatched farmhouse. Built pre-1838. In farmyard. Direct-entry plan. Gabled oaten straw roof. Rendered brick chimneys. Rendered stone walls. Replacement timber windows. Timber and glazed door in flat-roofed two-bay porch. One bay has collapsed in.

82 **Derryiron, near Rhode** **House**

Detached three-bay single-storey thatched farmhouse. Built pre-1838. In farmyard at end of short avenue. Hipped oaten straw roof. Rendered walls. Single-storey outbuildings.

USEFUL ADDRESSES

1. General

a. Grant assistance for thatched buildings

i. Housing Grants Section, Department of the Environment, Heritage and Local Government, Government Offices, Ballina, Co. Mayo. Telephone: (1890) 305030 [Lo-call] or (096) 24200.
ii. Heritage Council, Kilkenny. Telephone: (056) 7770777. Fax: (056) 7770788. Email: heritage@ heritage.iol.ie Web: www.heritagecouncil.ie

b. Grant assistance for general repairs to Protected Structures

i. County Council Conservation Officer or Planning Section
ii. Heritage Council, Kilkenny. Telephone: (056) 7770777. Fax: (056) 7770788. Email: heritage@ heritage.iol.ie Web: www.heritagecouncil.ie

c. Advice on alterations, etc. to Protected Structures and other historic buildings

i. County Council Conservation Officer or Planning Section
ii. Architectural Heritage Advisory Service, Department of the Environment, Heritage and Local Government, Dún Scéine, Harcourt Lane, Dublin 2. Tel: (01) 4117100. Fax: (01) 4781335.

d. Information on architectural heritage

i. Department of Irish Folklore, University College Dublin, Belfield, Dublin 4. Telephone: (01) 7168216.
ii. Heritage Council, Kilkenny. Telephone: 056–7770777. Fax: (056) 7770788. Email: heritage@ heritage.iol.ie Web: www.heritagecouncil.ie
iii. Irish Architectural Archive, 73 Merrion Square, Dublin 2. Telephone: (01) 6763430. Fax: (01) 6616309. Note: after about August 2004, the address will be 45 Merrion Square, Dublin 2. Email: info@iarc.ie. Web: www.iarc.ie
iii. Museum of Country Life, Turlough Park, Castlebar, Co. Mayo. Telephone: (1890) 687386. Email: tpark@museum.ie
iv. National Inventory of Architectural Heritage (NIAH), Dún Scéine, Harcourt Lane, Dublin 2. Telephone: (01) 4117100. Fax (01) 4781335. Email: wcumming@duchas.ie
v. National Museum of Ireland (Museum of Country Life)
    See above under Museum of Country Life
vi. www.thatch.org

2. Thatchers

i. The local authority Conservation Officer or Planning Section may have a list of thatchers.
ii. Talk to other owners of thatched buildings – they are by far the best guide.

3. Suppliers of straw, reed, scollops, etc.

As for previous section.

General books on vernacular architecture

Danaher, Kevin, *Ireland's Vernacular Architecture*. Cork (Mercier Press) 1975. Re-issued by Bord Fáilte in colour as *Ireland's Traditional Houses* (1991).

Evans, E. Estyn, *Irish Folkways*. London (Routledge) 1957.

Gailey, Alan, *Rural Houses of the North of Ireland*. Edinburgh (John Donald) 1984.

Ní Fhloinn, Bairbre and Dennison, Gabriel (editors), *Traditional Architecture in Ireland and its role in rural tourism and development*. Dublin 1994.

Oliver, Paul (editor), *Encyclopedia of the Vernacular Architecture of the World*. Oxford (Cambridge University Press) 1997.

Oliver, Paul, *Dwellings. The vernacular house world wide*. London (Phaidon Press) 2003.

Rudofsky, Bernard, *Architecture without Architects*. Albuquerque (University of New Mexico Press) 1987.

Shaffrey, Patrick and Maura, *Irish Countryside Buildings*. Dublin (O'Brien Press) 1985.

Guidelines for thatch

Department of the Environment, *Conservation Guidelines No. 10. Roofs and Rainwater Goods*. Dublin no date.

Environment Service, Department of the Environment for Northern Ireland, *Technical Note No. 2. Thatch*. Belfast 1994.

Society for the Protection of Ancient Buildings and the Rural Development Commission, *Technical Pamphlet 10. The Care and Repair of Thatched Roofs*. London 1986. Authors Peter Brockett and Adela Wright.

Reports, studies and articles in journals

Aalen, F. H. A., Whelan, K. and Stout, M. (editors), *Atlas of the Irish Rural Landscape*. Dublin (Royal Irish Academy) 1997.

Buchanan, Ronald H., 'Thatch and thatching in north-east Ireland', *Gwerin*, 1 (1957), pp. 123–42.

Dennison, Gabriel and Ó Floinn, Bairbre, *A Lost Cause? A review of the present state of thatch and thatching in Ireland with proposals for the 1990s*. Dublin 1990.

Environment and Heritage Service, *Historic Thatch (Ireland) Study: Interim Report*. Belfast 1997.

Fitzsimons, Jack, *Bungalow Bashing*. Kells 1990.

— 'Thatched Roofs', *Bungalow Bliss*, 1981 edition, pp. 408–14.

Heritage Council, *Irish Thatched Roofs: is their future a thing of the past?* Kilkenny 1999.

— *Policy Paper on Irish Thatched Roofs and the National Heritage*. Kilkenny 2002.

ICOMOS, *Charter on the Built Vernacular Heritage*. Mexico 1999.

Mogey, J. M., 'Thatch', *Ulster Folklife*, 3 (1940), pp. 134–7.

Mulhausen, Ludwig, 'Contributions to the study of the tangible material culture of the Gaoltacht', *Journal of the Cork Historical and Archaeological Society*, 38 (1933), pp. 67–71 and 39 (1934), pp. 41–51.

Ní Fhloinn, Bairbre and Dennison, Gabriel, *Traditional Architecture in Ireland and its role in rural tourism and development*. Dublin 1994.

Ó Danachair, Caoimhín, 'The flail in Ireland', *Ethnologia Europaea*, 4 (1970), pp. 50–55.

— 'The Questionnaire System: roofs and thatching', *Béaloideas*, 15 (1945), pp. 203–17.

O'Neill, Timothy P., *Life and Tradition in Rural Ireland*. London (Dent & Sons Ltd) 1977.

O'Reilly, Barry, *Towards a National Policy on Vernacular Architecture*. Report for the Heritage Council. Unpublished 1995.

Reeners, Roberta (compiler/editor). *A Wexford Farmstead. The conservation of an 18th-century farmstead in County Wexford*. Kilkenny (The Heritage Council) 2003.

Studies and local histories for Offaly

Byrne, Michael, 'Tullamore: the growth process, 1785–1841', in Nolan, William and O'Neill, Timothy P. (editors), *Offaly: History and Society*. Dublin (Geography Publications) 1998, pp. 569–626.

Craig, Maurice, *Preliminary Report of Survey of Areas of Historic and Artistic Interest in County Offaly*. Dublin (An Foras Forbartha) 1973.

Garner, William, *Tullamore: Architectural Heritage*. Dublin (An Foras Forbartha) 1980.

Heaney, Paddy, *At the Foot of Slieve Bloom: history and folklore of Cadamstown*. Kilcormac Historical Society. No date.

Kearney, John, *Killeigh and Geashill: a pictorial record*. Tullamore (Esker Press) 1990.

Kilcormac Historical Society, *Kilcormac–Killoughey Parish Album*. Ferbane 1996.

Leamanaghan Parish Millennium Committee. *A Pilgrim People: stories from Leamanaghan Parish*. 1999.

Mac Mahon, Noel, *In the Shadow of the Fairy Hill: Shinrone and Ballingarry – a history*. Shinrone 1998.

Moloney, Aonghus, Jennings, David, Keane, Margaret and McDermott, Conor, *Irish Archaeological Wetland Unit Transactions Volume 2: Excavations at Clonfinlough, Co. Offaly*. Dublin (UCD) 1993.

Nolan, William and O'Neill, Timothy P. (editors), *Offaly: History and Society*. Dublin (Geography Publications) 1998.

O'Brien, Caimin and Sweetman, David, *Archaeological Inventory of County Offaly*. Dublin (Stationery Office) 1997.

O'Reilly, Barry, *Thatch in County Offaly: a report for Offaly County Council*. November 2002.

Offaly County Council, *County Development Plan 1996*. Tullamore. September 1996.

Sheehy, Margaret, 'Architecture in Offaly', *Journal of the County Kildare Archaeological Society*, 14 (1964–70), pp. 23–8.

Tullamore Urban District Council, *Tullamore Town Development Plan 1997*. Tullamore April 1997.

Wrafter, Sr Oliver, *Rahan Looks Back*. Rahan 1989.

Department of Irish Folklore Manuscript Collection
IFC Ms 1772, pp. 364–391 and pp. 395–405.

Folktales of the Irish Countryside

Kevin Danaher

Nowadays there is a whole generation growing up who cannot remember a time when there was no television; and whose parents cannot remember a time when there was no radio and cinema. It is not, therefore, surprising that many of them wonder what people in country places found to do with their time in the winters of long ago.

People may blink in astonishment when reminded of the fact that the night was often too short for those past generations of country people, whose own entertainment with singing, music, dancing, cards, indoor games and storytelling spanned the evenings and into morning light.

Kevin Danaher remembers forty of the stories that enlivened those past days. Some are stories told by members of his own family; others he took down in his own countryside from the last traditional storytellers. Included are stories of giants, of ghosts, of queer happenings and of the great kings of Ireland.

Things Irish

Anthony Bluett

Things Irish provides the reader with an entertaining and informative view of Ireland, seen through the practices, beliefs and everyday objects that seem to belong specifically to this country. Discarding the usual format of chapters on a variety of themes, the book uses short descriptive passages on anything from whiskey to standing stones, from May Day to hurling, in order to create a distinctive image of Irish life. The reader is free to roam from topic to topic, from passage to passage, discovering a wealth of new and surprising facts and having a number of misguided beliefs put right.

In Ireland Long Ago

Kevin Danaher

Those who have only the most hazy idea of how our ancestors lived in Ireland will find enlightenment in these essays which range widely over the field of Irish folklife. Kevin Danaher describes life in Ireland before the 'brave new world' crept into the quiet countryside. Or perhaps 'describe' is not the right word. He rather invites the reader to call on the elderly people at their homes, to listen to their tales and gossip and taste their food and drink; to step outside and marvel at their pots and pans, ploughs and flails; to meet a water diviner; to join a faction fight; hurry to a wedding and bow down in remembrance of the dead.

In this book Kevin Danaher has not only given us a well balanced picture of life in Ireland, but has also gone far to capture the magic of the written word.